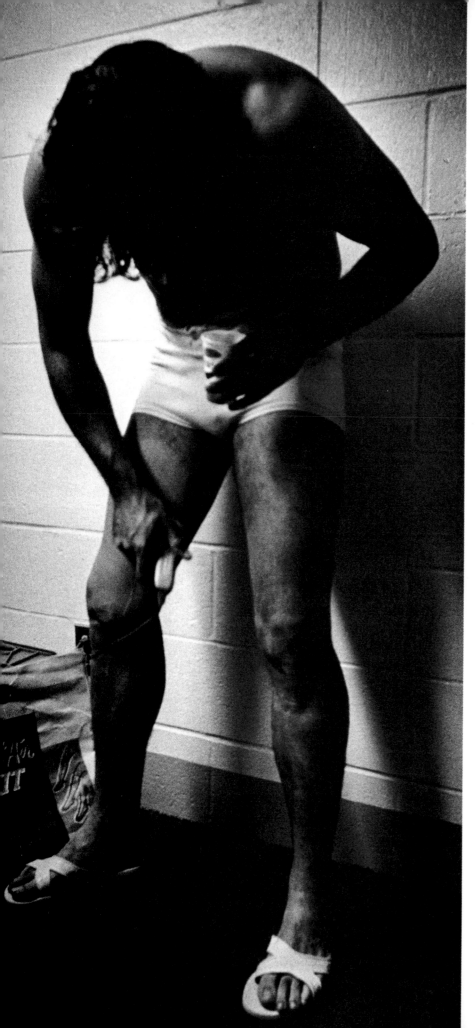

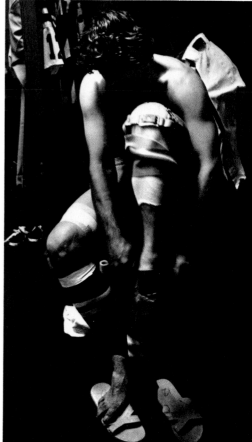

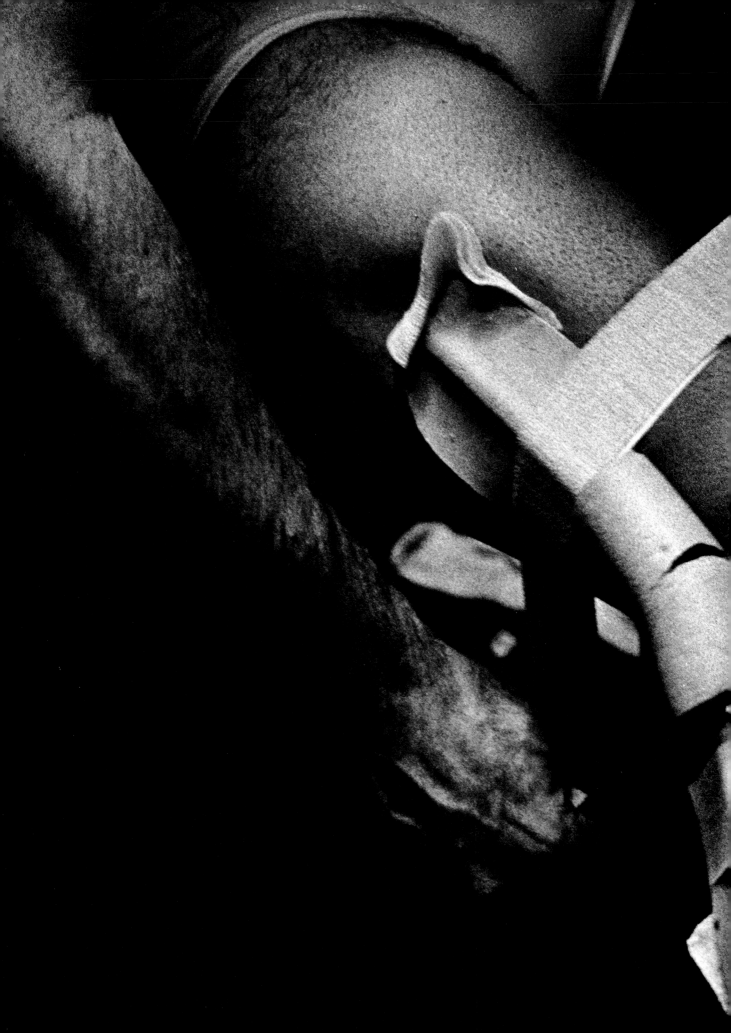

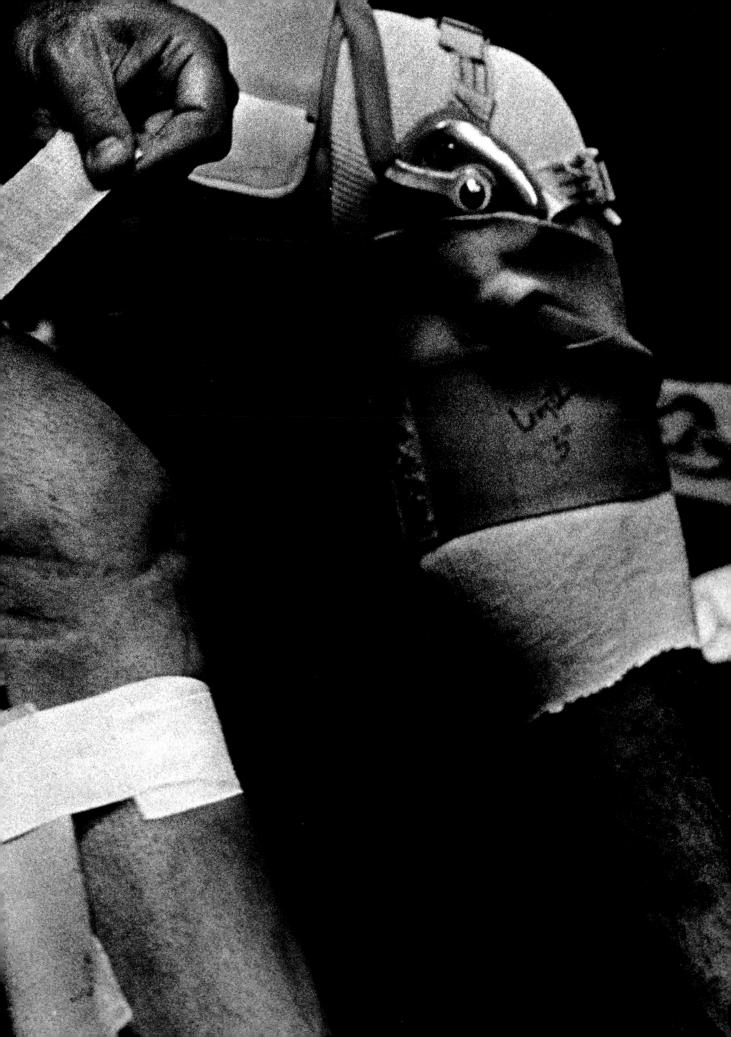

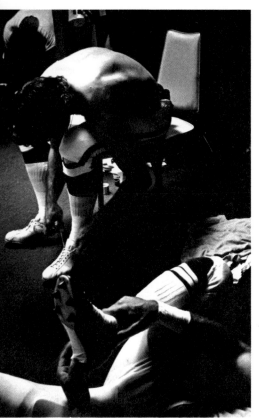

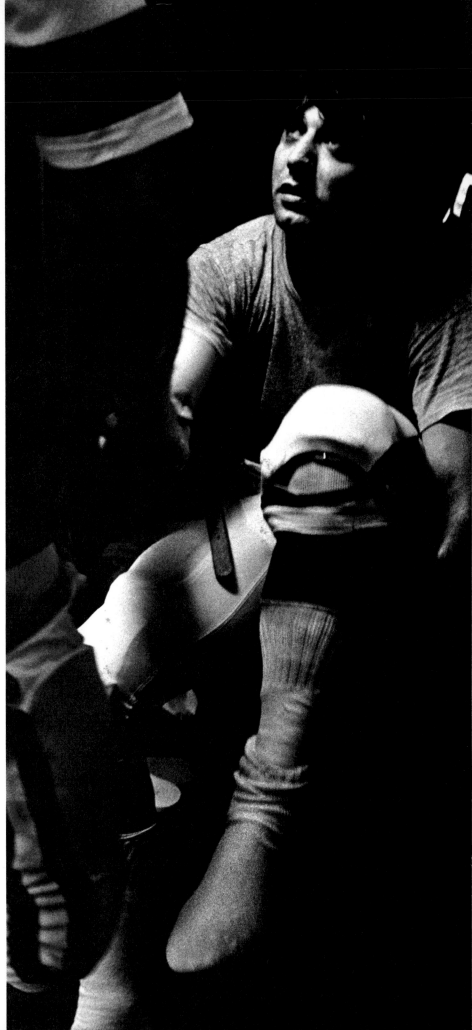

"When I come out on
 the field, I'm ready to
 roll. And the way
 I want to do it playing
 football is the same
 way I want to be in
 daily life. I want to
 be smooth. I want to
 operate with no excess
 motion or disturb-
 ances. It's a matter
 of style."

JOE NAMATH A MATTER OF STYLE

WITH
BOB OATES, JR.

Little, Brown and Company
Boston, Toronto

ACKNOWLEDGMENTS

Joe does some talking about the importance of teamwork in this book and I can't think of a better example of what he is talking about than the book itself. A volume of this sort takes the coordinated efforts of scores of talented people. If you would like to get a feel for how the work has been produced, read the list of people to whom Joe and I are happily indebted.

First, is Jim Walsh, Joe's friend and official counselor, whose enthusiasm, understanding and support allowed us to function as friends instead of partners and kept me afloat in heavy times. Next are Jim Trecker, Frank Ramos and all the officials and players on the New York Jets who rendered timely assistance and withstood my intrusions cheerfully.

The photographers have been so important to this project that they have received a special page. For help on the manuscript I am beholden to Lee Hutson, John Wiebusch, Tom Bennett and especially my father, Bob Oates, Sr.

Transcribing of the tapes and retyping the manuscript were chores handled by Roz Cole and Rhonda Casman. Supplying ideas, holding my hand and giving me timely kicks were all accomplished by Jack Wrobbel, Mike Gaines and Bill Von Torne.

Typesetting for a book like this is an exact craft and it was handled beautifully and unbelievably quickly by Harry Wollman and the staff at Fotoset in Los Angeles. And given all the photographs, the people who make the pictures of the pages from which the printing plates are made become very important. These people are Dave Gardner and his group at Gardner-Fullmer Lithograph in Buena Park, California. The printing of the book itself was handled with great courtesy and concern by Kingsport Press in Tennessee.

We received truly outstanding help from the people at Little, Brown. Charles Everitt is the type of editor I need — supportive and intelligently critical both. He and Peter Carr, the production expert, suffered my indignities gracefully and helped the project immensely.

The designers have been left for last because they have had the greatest impact on the book as you see it. To Dave Boss I am grateful not only for passing his hands over the work at critical stages, making the rough seem smooth, but also for making my last few years an education in sports publishing. And then a great thanks to Dave Johnston, who worried every page into final shape. Dave could make the telephone book look good and have it for you in the morning if you needed it. He, Steven Escalante, and assorted friends and relations churned out the design mechanicals for this book in a creative storm.

Working with all these people has been a lot of fun. I just wish I could blame them for the mistakes I have managed to slip in here despite them.
Bob Oates, Jr.
March 11, 1973
Jai Guru Dev

Editor: Charles Everitt
Designer: David Johnston;
    Johnston and Escalante;
    Los Angeles
Design Consultant: David Boss
Photography Consultant: Bob Engle
Production Manager: Peter Carr
Typesetting: Fotoset; Los Angeles
Filming: Gardner-Fullmer Lithograph;
    Buena Park, California
Printing: Kingsport Press;
    Kingsport, Tennessee

Library of Congress Cataloging in Publication Data

Namath, Joe Willie, 1943-
    A matter of style.

    1. Namath, Joe Willie, 1943-   2. Football.
I. Oates, Bob, joint author. II. Title.
GV939.N28A32   796.33'2'0924 [B]   73-4992
ISBN 0-316-59690-6

T09/73

Published simultaneously in Canada by Little, Brown & Company (Canada) Limited
Printed in the United States of America

PHOTOGRAPHY

Football is a visually exciting sport, Joe Namath is a photogenic man and this book is in part a photographic album. To capture Joe's many moods and quick motions, we employed some of the outstanding photographers in the country. Most of the photography in this book was specially commissioned and shot to order by skilled craftsmen. A special thanks is due to Bob Engle for his role as a consultant on photographers.

Special equipment was used in two cases. The cover and a four-page color portfolio inside were taken by Johnny Zimmerman using stroboscopic equipment. Each of the many images in a stroboscopic photograph is lit for one brilliant micro-instant by equipment that costs $6,000. Zimmerman was prepared to capture eighteen images in one second, but Joe doesn't take that long to throw.

All of the black-and-white sequence photographs of Joe throwing the ball were taken by Walter Iooss, Ken Regan and Jay Spencer using a machine known as a Hulscher camera. Although we only shot at ten frames a second, the camera is capable of running fifty frames in that time—each a perfect thirty-five millimeter picture. Pictures from this camera revealed aspects of Namath's motion which he didn't know himself.

Photographers usually disappear behind their cameras. Here are the people who made this book a visual experience.

Harry Benson
One of America's most respected photo-journalists, a frequent assignee on assignments presidential and royal

Larry Fried
Has had more covers on "Newsweek" than any other photographer; winner of the Overseas Press Club award for photography

Walter Iooss
A first-string "Sports Illustrated" photographer known for his gutty pictures, his Dutch girl friend Evelyn and his dog Waldo

Ken Regan
Frequent contributor and cover photographer for "Newsweek," "Time," "New York Times Magazine" and many European magazines

Barton Silverman
Staff photographer for the New York Times, the New York News Photographer of the Year in 1970, and a master of black-and-white football action

Jay Spencer
One of Florida's best photographers, a frequent contributor to publications of NFL Properties

Herb Weitman
A teacher of photography at Washington University in St. Louis, the St. Louis Cardinals' team photographer and a craftsman who could probably get Haley's comet in focus

Johnny Zimmerman
A major contributor to "Life" (R. I. P.) and "Sports Illustrated"; a rare combination of talents both in-person and in the studio

Other contributing photographers: David Boss, Tim Culek, Malcolm Emmons, Dan Farrell, Bob Glass, Bob Gomel, T. Makita, Victor Mikus, Richard Raphael, Russ Reed, Russ Russell, R. H. Stagg, Joe Van Mill, Lou Witt

foreword

Joe Namath has his own style. On the field and off, he's a man who does things his own way.

Before we started work on this book, the only element of his style that was personally familiar to me was his way of throwing a football. It seemed to me then as it does now that his throwing motion is a breakthrough—the application of centrifugal motion to the art of passing.

But it wasn't until I started working with him that I began to see that he had his own style in other aspects of football, too, in mechanical things like the drop-back and ball handling, as well as in more theoretical areas such as play-calling and leadership. And it took more than working with him, it took living and drinking and clowning and hassling, before I began to see that his approach to football is tied directly to his style of living away from the game. Joe has thought out his moves both on and off the field and has arrived at basic ways of functioning which feel good to him—ways that feel easy and comfortable.

And he makes good use of the methods he has developed. Even though a football field is a wild place, full of intense man-to-man struggles and full-speed collisions, Namath can usually glide smoothly through the action using techniques that are efficient, uncomplicated and fluid. And even though his life off the field can be a demanding combination of distractions, starting with his football responsibilities and continuing through business operations, television, movies, newspapers, and an incessant stream of insistent strangers, he manages to weave through the obstacles in ways which are, again, efficient, uncomplicated and fluid. Both playing and living, he makes it look easy most of the time.

When I first came to him with the idea for this book, I wasn't sure that he was a man with a conscious understanding of his actions on the football field. I wanted to do a book on quarter-backing, but for all I knew he was a superb natural athlete who simply went out and did it the way he felt it. But it turned out he was not only aware of what he was doing, he was also nearly as enthusiastic as I was about the possibilities his style would have for other quarterbacks.

I was glad he felt that way. I had hoped the project would make sense to him, even though I knew he couldn't possibly be as emotionally involved in it as I was. It couldn't excite him unduly because his style had evolved gradually over the course of more than twenty years, and for him it was natural and normal. But for me the centrifugal throwing motion had come with the sudden force of a revolution, and the exhilarating effect had left me with the crusading zeal of a convert.

You see, the idea for this book first came to me on the practice field of a semi-pro football team, the New York Rams, as I struggled through the delicious strain of trying to become a pocket passer. I had been working to accomplish this feat for more than a decade with results that would have been discouraging to a more balanced personality when I changed my life by moving to New York City. Here I had the opportunity of watching the quarterback of the New York Jets ten times a year on television, and somehow, through great green clouds of envy, the faintest glint of salvation began to appear.

Joe Namath didn't look like other quarterbacks I had ever seen. He didn't step forward as he passed and then follow through straight ahead. He stepped out to the side a little and turned around to his left. Sometimes he wound up running *away* from the line of scrimmage instead of moving toward it. It looked a little odd, but it also looked as if it were simpler and quicker than anything I was used to seeing. With the desperation of a fantasy quarterback in exile at wide receiver, I jumped on this faint hope and began to remake my throwing motion.

It took awhile. I didn't have the benefit of any coaching and Joe moved so fast when he threw the ball that it was hard to pick up details. But as I kept working, I found that the logic of his circular throwing motion tended to solve some problems by itself.

Of course, no physical technique can solve all problems. I still had my congenital deficiencies in such areas as coordination and courage, but there was one important difference. I also had a job as a starting quarterback.

I've played four seasons now, four crazy autumns with a zany team, and the fun I have had makes all those years of waiting worthwhile. And through these four seasons, as I watched myself

Quarterback, New York Jets

Quarterback, New York Rams

improve, as I looked on amazed while yet another sideline pass arrived in reasonably good shape, the idea for this book gradually took shape. It was a natural. I knew that people would listen to Joe Namath when he told them how to throw a football, since he is arguably the best quarterback ever and surely the best at this time. And I knew from personal experience that what he had to say was a genuine contribution.

As I drove out to find him at Shea Stadium one November afternoon, there were only two things bothering me. One, as I say, was the question of how much he actually knew about what he was doing. The other was much more basic, and had to do with questions of personality. I was scared silly.

Both difficulties disappeared almost immediately. In our first conversation in the Jets' locker room, as Joe strained against a weight machine to rebuild his injured left knee, I found that he was not only aware of those overall aspects of his motion that I had been able to pick up, but that he also had detailed knowledge in areas that had never occurred to me, areas such as his uncluttered arm action and his unusual use of weight distribution.

And in that same conversation, I found out that he wasn't going to give me anything to be afraid of. Joe Namath is a nice guy. He has that beautiful smile and strangers see it as often as friends and judging by other reputations, at least, he has to be one of the easiest of America's

heroes to meet and work with.

We worked together for six or seven months in Vermont, New York and California, and the whole experience was one of the most pleasant I have had. Neither of us is a fiend for hard work but if our approach was casual for the most part, the result turned out even better than I had hoped—and I had hoped for quite a lot. There were two reasons for this. In the first place, as we lived and worked together I found that I was at least as interested in the way Joe handles his head, on and off the field, as I was about the way he plays football. He has been under some unusual pressures in the last ten years and it is clear that he has been able to learn from his experiences and modify his feelings and behavior in such a way that he can handle his responsibilities while maintaining a comfortable and very private personal life. I know it felt good to be around him and I was fascinated by his conscious understanding of the way to keep the good feeling happening. In the first part of the book we have included some conversations that consider his ideas on his personal style.

In the second place, when the deadline got close and his words went down in cold type, Joe leaned in over the manuscript and pored over it line by line. In every section, he added and subtracted words, lines and whole paragraphs, sometimes to my temporary chagrin but definitely to the betterment of the final product. Most of the words in this book are Joe's, and they are not all transcribed from tape recordings.

contents

"I'm a happy guy,
basically. I usually
enjoy what I'm doing.
And believe it or not,
I'm somewhat con-
servative. I want to do
things with confidence
and style, but I don't
want to make waves.
If I don't cause any
problems, I don't have
to do any worrying—
and I don't like to
worry."

1 real life

He is Broadway Joe, after all, Joe Willie White Shoes, and I suppose I expected to find him bright-light flamboyant, racing full speed with the jet set. An itinerary of a typical off-season month tends to uphold that image, too. He's in Hollywood doing the Sonny and Cher show one week, in Vegas gambling lightly and golfing a lot the next; he's in Puerto Rico in a pro-am tournament on Tuesday, back to Hollywood Sunday, and gone to Spain for a yachting expedition by the following Saturday night.

But somehow in person he doesn't come off as a hard-edged swinger, and being with him doesn't feel frenetic and fast-paced. He may move around a lot, but he manages to do it while moving slowly, easing from place to place in a smooth and comfortable way. He doesn't make a big splash coming into a scene and he doesn't make a lot of waves leaving. In fact, he sometimes seems shy in a crowd of people, sitting quietly and smiling while those around him carry the entertainment load.

I spent my first month with him in Vermont, where he was running a boys' football camp, and in Hempstead, Long Island, at the training camp of the New York Jets, and in that time his quiet and courteous manner fooled me a little. He seemed so

calm and low-key that I began to wonder if his charismatic image was an accident of his photogenic face and the power of the New York press.

But as the season came nearer and his responsibilities increased, a different side of Namath's personality started to appear. He might be lying comfortably in his room at ten to noon, sipping a coke and jiving with his friends, but at straight-up twelve he would be running a press conference with a lively humor born of full confidence. He might be deferential in certain social situations, but when the games started, he would be the authoritative leader of his team.

It was an amazing phenomenon to me, his ability to become what the time required of him, and I began to see there are a number of sides to his personality. He can function well in a wide variety of circumstances and he can relate to nearly any type of person, including cab drivers, newsmen, politicians, cronies, celebrities, small children and expanding matrons.

It is probably this flexibility, this ability to move from place to place in his head, that caused a good deal of the sensation when Namath first became a big name

five years ago. Not everybody understood how he could party on Saturday night and win a Super Bowl on Sunday. But that's who he is, and his distinctive personal style is a result of the way he manages to combine his various facets into a coherent whole.

There is little doubt that he has mellowed some in the last several years. I didn't know him in those early seasons in New York, but all the smoke that appeared around him must have concealed some fire at least. Even now the embers glow brightly. He is an emotional man who does more on-field stomping around than the usual quarter-back. He can be testy in the locker room after an unpleasant game and he can get irritated and snap at people who seem to be adding to his grief after one of his longer days.

But emotional outbursts are not the rule for Joe now, if they ever were. In fact, his limitations in general are not very interesting. He has his fair share, but the interesting thing is not his particular set of limits but how well he functions within them. More than most people I have met, he knows his head and he knows his feelings and he knows how he has to act to keep things moving comfortably. He manages to do it most of the time.

Joe Namath is throwing the ball easily through the soft summer air of Vermont. He is surrounded by children, young football players from eight to eighteen dressed in catch-all uniforms with ill-fitting pads and mismatched socks.

They have just finished their second practice of the day and many of them are heading heavily up the hill toward showers and dinner, but some have stayed behind, standing with their helmets in hand or kneeling down on one leg, and they are watching Namath catch the ball casually, put it up beside his ear and sail it again far downfield.

This is Joe Namath's Football Camp for Boys. It says so on a hand-painted sign in front of the funky ski lodge that sits on top of the hill, a fading barn-red building that takes in summer boarders who crunch through the halls in football cleats while it waits for the snow to reassert itself late in the fall.

Football could not be played in a setting of more natural beauty. A shallow valley curves down and away from the lodge, beginning at the bottom of the slope with a wide, comfortable meadow. Out on this meadow, wooden goal posts have been placed a hundred yards apart, more or less; and on the field that is suggested between the poles the children have spent a month running through happy approximations of the more machine-like football practices that will open all over the country in a few weeks.

It has been a month of fun and learning for the kids and a

month of tension-free self-satisfaction for Namath and his teaching staff of pro players and coaches. Joe is not an assertive, holler-guy type as a coach, but he has obviously enjoyed his quiet conferences with young quarterbacks and the small three- and four-man drills he has put them through. Helping youngsters improve themselves is not a bad way to spend a summer vacation, and the kids provide the kind of meal-time conversation close to the heart of any football man. There is Eddie, the big red-headed quarterback with the unflappable manner and quick delivery. There is John, the twelve-year-old from Alabama who already has the crossfield cut down cold. There is little Eric, the halfback who is ten years old and looks eight and runs like a bug escaping a squashing.

But now it is late in the last week and the reality of other fields and other players is beginning to intrude itself into the New England idyll. Joe has been working on his arm all month—all spring actually—and now he is letting it loose on long passes to a friend of his, a pool-playing buddy from New York who is standing forty and then fifty and then sixty yards away.

It is a classic sight, the great quarterback in the summer country. Comfortable in a sleek

green sweat suit with white stripes around the shoulders and down the legs, he moves lightly through the elegant motion that casts the ball away. The kids are watching and Joe is feeling good, feeling the power that is in him, stretching to his limits in Vermont in July. His friend is out there seventy yards by now, and he has given up on catching the ball. As it soars, he circles warily, then surrounds it when it lands, and relays it back upfield.

Ball in hand, Namath is ready for his final throw. It will be a bravura performance. He sets himself facing square straight ahead with his feet lined up even and spread shoulder width. He smiles down the meadow to his apprehensive friend, coils the top of his body and without lifting his feet he flips the ball high and tightly spinning, splitting the air, and chases the guy out from under the landing spot.

"I enjoyed that," Joe says later. "It feels good to be able to put the ball out that way."

Weren't you worried about hurting your arm throwing like that without taking a step?

"No. I don't like to worry in the first place, I don't like the feeling, so I hardly ever do any worrying. And there's no reason for me to be concerned about my arm because I know what I can do with a football. I know I can throw that kind of pass as long as I'm warm and my arm is good and loose. Knowing my limits is basic to my job because a quarterback has to know what passes he can throw and what passes he can't."

What passes can't you throw?

"Talking about passes I'd use in a game, there aren't any. If a guy is seventy yards out there when I'm getting set to throw, the ball won't reach him because by the time it comes down he's going to be a hundred yards. But anything in reason, I can throw it. Deep outs, long balls, passes over the middle—I know where I'm throwing the ball and I rarely put it where I don't want it. Unless I'm off balance or the ball slips in my hand."

Maybe that's just confidence but it sounds like ego.

"I'm not ego tripping. I know where I'm at, is all. We're talking about football here, you know, not real estate or acting. Football, hell, I've been playing football twenty-three years. I ought to know what I'm doing. And it's a good feeling having control over the ball like that. Sometimes in games I can't really see what happens on some passes but then we'll be looking at films and I'll see something I threw. Maybe there's a guy on one side of my receiver and a guy on the other side and that ball just slips right in there between them. That's nice. 'Wow, I threw that,' I'm saying. It's a good feeling. Or maybe I'm at practice and a couple of guys are out there talking fifty yards away and I can take the ball and put it right where I want it, scare them with it or something. That's fun, you know, throwing the football straight is fun."

You seem to be the type of guy who enjoys himself a lot.

"It's true. I'm not really sure why it is, but for some reason I've had a happy attitude my whole life. Maybe it was the blood my parents gave me, or the stars I was born under, I don't know. But most times I'm happy with the things I do. I usually have a good time, even if I'm just sitting around talking to my friends or whatever."

And that extends to playing football?

"Of course. I've been playing football practically my whole life and so some parts of it, meetings and stuff like that, that gets a little old. But talking about playing quarterback, boy, quarterback is a gas. It's a hell of a position to play. It's a big responsibility, a challenge, and I like that. I get a lot of self-satis-faction out of it. First off, you have to be a pretty damn good athlete to be quick enough, have the right footwork and a good arm, have good enough reactions. And then you have to be able to handle the tactics, call the right plays in the right situations, keep calm under pressure and keep your team together and working. It's fun moving down the field and getting points on the board. I get a charge out of it.

Sounds like you would play the game just for fun.

"That's wrong. You hear people say the game's so much fun somebody would play it even if he weren't getting paid for it. But that doesn't make any sense to me, not in the pros. The

athletes are so big and fast the game is too dangerous to play just for the hell of it. Every week one of your friends is limping off the field or getting carried off and that has to make you stop and think. And then there's all the time it takes, the mental strain it puts on you week after week, the pressure it puts on the family life for married guys. Let's put it this way: if they tried to run the National Football League on fun alone, I don't think they could field one team."

When you are playing, do you enjoy yourself more against the tough teams or the weaker ones?

"You can give me those bottom teams every time. Not that they can't beat you, but playing the solid teams, playing Miami or Oakland or Washington, that's work, buddy. That's a tense way to spend time. One screw-up can blow the whole thing and you don't ever get to relax and run a comfortable game. Playing quarterback is my job, after all, and I don't mind working. But if I can do my job and, at the same time, be a little more relaxed, a little more easy about it, that's the way I like it best."

Do you think other teams point for Joe Namath, psyche themselves up to play against you?

"I hope so. I don't know that they do, but if they did, it would make me feel good. I'd be glad to know they thought that much of me. But as far as making it tough on me, they don't really have to do anything special. Defenses are getting so tough these days they don't need any unusual incentive. Football is a progressive game. It keeps getting

finer and finer. The players get stronger and faster and the coaching gets more sophisticated and every year it gets a little more difficult to get anything done out there. You just have to keep working and studying and try to stay a step ahead."

Later on we're going to be talking about your offensive strategy. I suppose you won't want to give away any of the small details because that would just make it tougher on you.

"I hope it won't, but I'm not going to hide anything. Hell, even defensive players should be able to read this book and learn something, learn how we try to work on them. It's all for the good of the game."

It's 8:30 in the morning, which is unlikely right there, and we are careening down one of the swerving highways in Vermont. Joe is at the wheel, his brother Frank is beside him and I'm in the back with Hoot Owl Hicks, Joe's good old friend from Alabama. It's a two-lane road and Joe is using both of them to get us over to Keane, New Hampshire, in time for a 9:30 flight back to the angular grey of New York City.

"I hate to hurry," Joe says. "I hate driving like this." But he keeps on doing it and nobody in the car gets to pay much attention to the last healthy scenery we'll see for quite some time.

It's 9:20 and we squeal into the airport parking lot. "I didn't

think we had a chance," Joe says, "I really didn't think we were going to make this thing."

We pull our bags out of the car, shoulder our way through the door and sprint across the floor to the ticket counter. But our big arrival scene stirs no action behind the counter. On the contrary, the girl takes her time telling us we're on our way to nowhere. The New York plane is not leaving at 9:30. It may not leave at all. It can't take off on the length of runway available when it has a full load—and today of course a full load is what it has. It's Sunday morning in Keane, New Hampshire, and we're stranded.

It's pretty funny. Joe makes a quick check of the facilities. "Damn," he says. "I don't mind waiting but I think this place is closed for the summer. The coffee shop is locked, the newspapers in that machine are all from last week. They don't even have a coffee machine."

Joe tries to charter a small plane to get us back but when the rental agent on the phone asks the question, "What day do you want it?" Joe knows it's all over. "I want it right *now*," he says, but he's laughing. That can't be arranged.

There's nothing to do but sit down on the linoleum, put our backs against the wall and get into it. "What's the use of being Joe Namath if you're going to get hung up like this?" asks Hoot Owl Hicks.

"I don't know," Joe says.

We made it to New York that afternoon.

"I hated that," Joe says later. "It wasn't the waiting that bothered me. We weren't going anywhere that day anyway. But rushing to an airport isn't the way I like to spend time. I don't like to hurry."

A man with knees like yours can't be expected to hurry much in any event.

"That's true. I had some speed once, back in college. I ran a 4.7 and 4.8 in the 40 with pads. Won a match race after practice one time against this speed merchant we got in from out West somewhere and he couldn't understand that at all. But I haven't been moving too fast here recently. Sometimes I can't even get up out of a chair too quickly. My leg will get stiff and I'll have to kind of ease it around and bend it slowly. But that's O.K. If I don't have a plane to catch, I'm hardly ever in a hurry."

When you are out on the field throwing a football you seem to be working pretty quickly.

"That's different. When I'm throwing a football everything is all out, full speed. The adrenalin starts pumping and everything just feels quick and sharp, everything happens immediately, right now. You go back, look and Boom! the ball's gone. It's a whole other world on the football field."

But don't you get that nervous edge when you are off the field? Don't you get nervous or worried sometimes and find yourself speeding up and getting jittery?

"No, it's like I was saying earlier. I hardly ever worry. I don't like it. I don't like the feeling of worrying, where your stomach is hurting and your mouth feels strange and your head's in a bad place. That's a bad feeling and I try to avoid it now. In the past, I did worry sometimes. I can remember times when it was really rough. Did you ever lose money that you couldn't afford to lose? I did that a couple of times when I was in school and, buddy, that's a bad feeling. It was just twenty or thirty cents, but it was money I was supposed to bring home.

"My mother sent me out to the store and it was change, and on the way home I'd go into the pool hall and a couple of times I lost it. I'd be walking home and my stomach would really be doing it to me, and all I could hope was that they'd forget about the change. But I knew they wouldn't. That was a bad way to feel, worrying like that."

Nobody likes to worry but a lot of times it's hard not to.

"If you don't like it, why do it? I think that at some point in your life you realize you don't have to worry if you do everything you're supposed to do right. Or if not right, if you do it the best you can. You have a job and you do your best on the job, then you don't have to worry about it. What can worry do for you? You are already doing the best you can. If your best isn't good enough, then you've got to find something else to do. At least I would. I wouldn't want to have

Living with bad knees

Injured on the sidelines can be a time for display of sartorial style.

a job I couldn't handle and be worrying all the time. I can play quarterback and I do that as well as I can and I don't worry about it. When it comes to business or taxes or something like that, I can't do those things as well as I play quarterback, so I get some help. I get the best help I can, and then I don't worry about those things either.

"I guess we all worry sometimes when we have a health problem, or a friend is in some kind of trouble. But I think that kind of worrying comes from the heart, not the head."

But other than that, you don't let things bother you anymore?

"Not much. Sometimes I'll be at a party and I'll be sitting there, and I'll catch myself thinking about the game coming up or some business conference I've got. But as soon as I catch myself, I just put it away. Why do I want to be worrying when I'm at a party? If I've already got my game plan down or my business options clear, why think about the situation until I'm confronted with it?"

How does this attitude carry over into your football? You have a reputation as a confident leader.

"Yeah, it's the same. If I'm prepared, I don't think about what I'm going to do until I have to. I know what I can do. I know what plays to use in what situations. Sometimes I'll be on the sideline and the other team will be lining up to punt and a coach will come over and ask me what play I'm going to run on first down. Hell, I'm not even thinking about it yet. I don't know where the ball will come down, which hashmark it will be on, whether my guy might run it back thirty yards. Maybe one of their defensive backs will get hurt covering the kick. I don't know the situation yet so I'm just waiting."

I'd like to know your thinking in a specific situation last season. This was your first call of the year, in the exhibition game against San Francisco. You hadn't played much in two years and the first thing that happened to you was a punt by the 49ers downed one foot from your goal line. On the first play you went back and threw a quick sideline pass to gain seven yards. That was a gutty call, I thought. It was almost like you were saying, 'Joe Namath is back.'

"Yeah, I remember that play. I remember the punt rolling toward the end zone and I'm saying, 'Get in there you sucker.' But then their guy leaped and batted it back and I said, 'O.K., then, that's a great play, that's all right.' But when I went out there, I mean there was only this much distance between the ball and the goal line. I was thinking over our plays but we don't have a single running play that couldn't lose a few inches depending on how the defense played it. There was nothing I could call and be sure of beforehand, so I didn't even call a play in the huddle."

What did you say in the huddle?

"I just said, 'Check with me.' We do that sometimes when I want to get up there and look the defense over before calling a play. This time I wanted to see what those guys thought we'd do. When I got up there, the linebacker on the left was up real tight and looked like he was going to blitz. The cornerback on that side was back a little, so I just called that quick out pattern to the left end. That's the way the situation was, so that's what I took."

You didn't worry about that play ahead of time?

"I don't call plays that I have to worry about."

Joe Namath shops at army surplus. This is two weeks after he has signed his new two-year contract for whatever you think it is, because I don't know, and he's out shopping at the army surplus. "You got any jeans?" he asks the man. "In the back," the guy says. Joe finds the type he likes, with horizontal pockets, and while he tries on a pair I rummage around in the $2 T-shirts, finding a couple I like. He carries out two pair of jeans and two shirts for $18 and that's really how he dresses a lot of the time—canvas shoes, old jeans, sweatshirts. He wears sweatshirts inside out. They say things like, "What You See Is What You Get," and, "It's Hard To Be Modest When You're As Great As I Am." People give them to him and he doesn't like the messages, but he hates to throw a good sweatshirt away.

I comment on his inexpensive taste. "Yeah, it's true," he says.

"Now this golf shirt I'm wearing, it did cost $14 when I got it. But that was four years ago. For $14 you better believe I'm not going to give up on the thing. It's a good shirt, nice and cool for the summertime, for golfing and things."

"But with the kind of money you've got, why don't you just go through clothes faster, keep yourself interested?"

"My mother wouldn't appreciate it."

When it's time to get into it, of course, Namath dresses with style. For all his well-publicized desire to do his own thing, he has a nice sense for the right thing to say and the right thing to wear, and a $900 investment in thirteen pairs of hand-tailored slacks is typical of the top end of his wardrobe.

The situation is similar with automobiles. He will hire a Cadillac limousine anytime he needs some wheels, but he also spends the summer and fall puttering around in a borrowed Toyota, grateful for the free transportation and totally oblivious of his proletarian image.

After the army surplus, as a matter of fact, it is the Toyota we get into for a ride to the next stop, a department store where Joe wants to pick up something in sportswear. So far the trip has gone smoothly, but this is where the mythic reality of Joe Namath asserts itself.

We go in the front door and make it to the escalators all right,

but there some young guy riding just in front of us says, "Either I'm really ripped or you're Joe Namath." "Naw," Joe says, and slouches off the top of the escalator. He turns into the sportswear department and stops, and that does it. He asks to see something and the saleslady asks for his autograph. Two others, a young man and woman, catch up at the same time, holding scraps of paper and scrambling for pens. I start to walk off, getting out of the way, and three more people pass me with bright eyes and the smile of a fisherman at a strike. Joe begins shuffling after me, signing and making small talk, heading for the escalator. Another wave catches him twenty feet from the top, but he signs his way through and steps on.

We glide down and at the bottom we pass a grandmother with an armful of shopping bags. She steps back quickly, like a bottle just broke in front of her. "I don't believe it," she says. By now the whole ground floor knows Joe has to return, and it seems like every face in the building is watching him make his escape. Normally, Joe is the kind of man who ambles along. He ambles. It's the perfect word. But right now he is ambling at a gallop, faster than I've ever seen him. "Hey, Joe," a girl calls to him from behind a counter, and he sort of half waves on the run. "I'd know that walk anywhere," the girl calls out. "Good luck!"

We make it out the door and stand on the sidewalk for a moment, savoring freedom. After considering the situation, he decides to give up on the clothes shopping and heads down the street to a supermarket. He's after some bleach and fabric softener to break his new jeans in, but the scene there is worse than in the department store. The express lane develops a ten-minute traffic jam as people come swarming from all over the store with brown bags, sales receipts and shopping lists, each one of them collecting a signature for somebody else, some friend or relative. One of the interesting autograph phenomena is that after the age of about fifteen or so, nobody ever asks for one for himself.

"My son Billy is your biggest fan," they say.

"It can be a hassle sometimes," Joe says, "signing my name over and over. I don't like crowds anyway. I don't like to be where there's a bunch of people crowded around me, in a lobby or an elevator or something. It has nothing to do with being a pro football player or signing autographs. I just don't like to feel closed in. I like to be able to get up and move. I like feeling free. So I try to get out of the autograph thing whenever I can without being mean to people. I take different routes walking around at training camp to try and shake the kids, things like that. But I don't make a big production out of it. It's nothing to complain about, really."

Why not? It restricts your life.

"Not much. It's easy to think of worse problems. Maybe I could have not even been able to sign autographs. I had a taste of that when I got my wrist broken a couple of years ago. Now that can be a problem. You can't use your good hand to do anything much and I'll tell you something else. I went through some pain with that sucker. I mean that thing hurt. It hurt me so bad sometimes I wanted to go and smash my arm against the wall, knock that cast into little pieces. Pain like that, that's a problem."

Is this the worst pain you've experienced?

"No, that wasn't bad at all next to the pain I had in my foot. That happened with this last knee operation. I came out of it with my knee in good shape considering, but my foot, buddy, that was something else. The nerve running alongside my knee got bruised or scraped or something and the pain got transferred to my foot. That thing used to throb and throb, it would just be hurting, hurting, hurting, until there were times I thought I was losing my mind. The pain came and went for months and it would get to me so bad I was a nervous wreck. It would be after me and I'd stop and say, 'All right now, Joe, damn it, this thing's hurting but you can't do anything about it. It could be cancer, you jerk, so just get it together. Try and relax, and be glad it's nothing serious.' And then it would give me a jolt right up my whole side. I'd try to tell myself it could be worse — and it could have been — even though there were times when

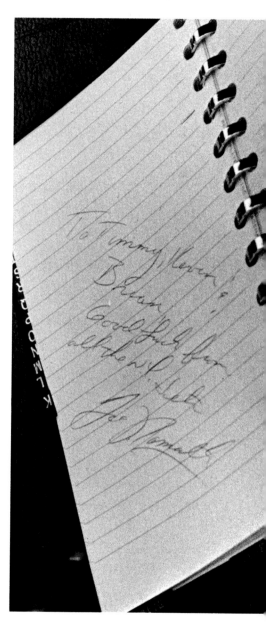

I'd be sitting there and the damn tears would come to my eyes. Boy, that thing would hurt."

There is a lot of pain involved in football. What do you think of the violent aspect of the game?

"I don't like it. It hurts, you know, and I'm not into pain particularly. I'm not a masochist. The guys playing this game get bigger and quicker every year and talking about just watching the game, I love to see them play. I was really sorry Bubba Smith got hurt last year because he's a good one, I enjoy watching him. But being out there on the field with those guys, that's rough. Us little dudes are always getting bent in half."

You must find it hard to stay calm, stand in the pocket, and throw the ball.

"It's weird. It's not a natural feeling at all, just standing there trying to pay attention to what's going on forty yards away and meanwhile here's all these cats trying to crunch you. It's not an easy thing to get used to. I noticed at the start of last year, after I hadn't played much in a couple of seasons, that I was having a little trouble getting adjusted again. The first couple of games in the exhibition season, I was a little nervous back there, a little jumpy. I was getting rid of the ball before I had to."

How do you get over that feeling?

"You just get used to it. The first time you get knocked down, it's kind of a shock. But you get yourself back together and throw a few more, and then you get hit again. The second one is not as bad as the first. And by the time you've been knocked down twenty times and got up twenty times, what difference does the twenty-first make? Hell, they can have you then. You've got a job to do. It gets to where you almost don't notice what's happening to you. I've had guys come up to me after the game and say, 'Man, you took a couple of shots out there,' And I'll say, 'What shots?' I don't remember getting hit. By the time I'm climbing up from going down I'm already thinking about the next play."

So you don't notice getting hit.

"Most of the time, no. But some hits stick with you pretty good. I still remember a lick I got in my first game after my knee injury in 1971 against San Francisco. I went back and threw a long pass. The ball was long gone and I'm just watching and it's bright and sunny and all of a sudden, Wham! it's dark and the stars are out and there's this whirring in my head. I mean I got hit. I didn't even know who did it. Boom! I got up and wobbled toward the line and said, 'Nice hit, buddy. That was a hell of a hit.' I got back into the huddle, bent over and started to get dizzy. I had to stand straight up and hitch at my pants a little

—take some air—before I could get myself going at all. A hit like that one, I'll remember that quite awhile."

I'm sure you will.

"Yeah, if you can just get up after a hit like that, you can't have too many problems. As long as I can walk, I'm not going to get too upset signing autographs, for instance. It usually takes only a few minutes anyway and I rarely get caught in it if I keep moving, keep walking, and don't stop where people have a chance to get themselves up into a crowd. And moving around isn't hard for me to do. I like it. I spend a lot of my life traveling."

What's the attraction in that for you?

"I like variety. I get bored if I stay in one place too long. I always like to move around and see what else is going on. I like changes even in little things. I've always got two or three toothbrushes and several kinds of toothpaste just so if I get up some morning and I don't feel like a hard brush right then, well, I've got a soft one."

What towns do you like the best?

"Los Angeles, Las Vegas, Tuscaloosa—and of course Fort Lauderdale, which is where I live some of the time.

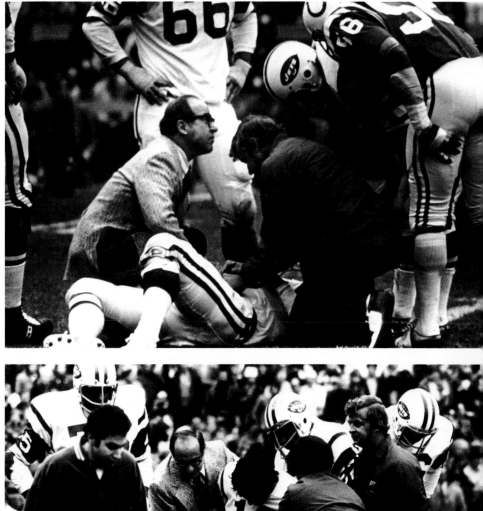

And what about New York. Do you like it there?

"If I didn't have to work there, I wouldn't be there much. What are you going to do during the day in New York? Where are you going to play golf? Or go out fishing or hunting? Or just lie on the beach? There's a lot of other places better for that plus they have places to go out and relax at night, so New York isn't any better that way, either."

Don't you ever feel you'd like to settle down—stay in one place, put down some roots?

"No, not yet. That's not how I feel, at least most of me. There's a part of me that would like the feeling of having family, children, a home—not just an apartment but a nice house with space around it—a place I'd always know I could go to. In fact, I was looking at a house in Tuscaloosa not too long ago. I'm still working toward a secure future for myself and hopefully a wife and children. But I thought about getting that house and then decided against it. It just isn't time yet. I'm still into traveling and seeing what's happening. I like Tuscaloosa but I like Florida, too. As soon as the season's over I get on a jet and get down to Ft. Lauderdale. There's no place in the world I like better than that but even Lauderdale after I've been there a few weeks is getting to me. I get on the phone to Tuscaloosa or try to set up some business in New York. When I think about it, think about what I wanted when I was a kid in Beaver Falls, I always did want to travel. When I first got to the pros and had some money I was jetting all over the country all the time. But now I've done that and once you've done what you've always wanted to, you don't have that drive, that need."

But you still travel.

"Yeah, but there's not the same push any more. Everything's casual. That's what it all is for me now—casual living. I get on the phone out to California and I tell the guy, 'Think of some place for dinner,' and I get on the plane and go. Get out there and for another $20 a limousine comes and picks me up and takes care of any hassles moving on the ground. There's no problems. It's just casual living."

A limousine seems like something of an extravagance.

"It's not, though. I began using them a few years ago. They don't cost much more than a taxi to the airport and I can stretch my legs out there in back and that makes it easier on my knees. I don't get a limousine if there's another way to do things, but I'll call one sooner than be hassled."

Jets and limousines can make the physical part easy, but I would think traveling would get to be a problem because you have to spend a lot of time in strange situations with people you don't know.

"I don't have that problem any more, but I know what you're talking about. I can remember times back when I was in school at Alabama and a couple of us would go from Tuscaloosa down to Lauderdale. I didn't like that at all, being alone in a big town full of people who don't know you from Adam. You go outside and you're lost. But that doesn't happen to me now. My publicity has made a difference. Now when I go anywhere in the country and I'm walking around people say, 'Hi, Joe, how you doing?' And I say, 'Hi,' and we talk a little and that's nice. I enjoy that because I like people. The autographs might be a bad part of this but it's nice to be able to go all over and people will make you feel at home, let you be comfortable. I can go anywhere now and I might not know exactly where I'm going, but I'm never lost. Somebody says, 'Hey' and I say, 'Hey. How you doing, buddy? Can you tell me where to go from here?' You know, 'Help me out.' And it's a gas, having people be friendly anywhere I am. I appreciate it."

That works here in this country. But how about when you get to Europe? You were over in Rome once doing a picture.

"Yeah, and it's just as easy to jump over there for a few days as it is to hop to California."

But over in Europe there aren't too many people who know about American football. People aren't going to recognize your face right away.

"That's true. I have to get into my wallet over there and see if they recognize Abe Lincoln and Andrew Jackson. I usually don't have much trouble."

There's a press conference called for noon. Joe has been working in training camp without a new contract. He doesn't intend to play without signing but he doesn't want to miss important practice time either. Now, in the week before the first game, he and the Jets have come to terms and the media people are heading out to Hofstra College, where the team is in residence. After several weeks of the grey training camp routine—meetings, practices, cafeteria cooking and more meetings—Joe Namath is about to inhabit his legend again.

The press conference will last less than an hour and it is Namath's special genius that when the occasion arises, he can live his myth. When the time comes for a public performance he gets into his upbeat personality as if it were a football suit. It's not that this part of him is a fake—it couldn't be faked—but he just doesn't need it during his normal daily existence.

Most of his life he keeps carefully sealed away from the pop cult that surrounds him. He is a country boy gone to be king in the big city and he lives his life true to his background rather than to his more recent pseudo-royal status. The game of pro football swirls around him, as do telecasters and sportswriters and gossip columnists and businessmen and advertisers and hangers-on and total strangers, but Joe manages to keep himself relatively unruffled because he

Jets' owner Phil Iselin announces a new contract for his famous passer

knows who he is and he knows what he likes. He is a man of few wants and simple pleasures and he would rather hang out with his friends than go out and dazzle an everwaiting world. When he went to Vermont for the football camp, he took along his brother Frank and his old-time Alabama friend, Hoot Owl Hicks, and the three lived together in a house in the hills. This was typical of Joe. Everywhere he goes, he carries his roots with him. He is a man who is rarely lost.

But now it's time to be the official Joe Namath—Joe Namath, No. 12 of the New York Jets; Joe Namath, media super hero. The commandeered dining room has been filled since 11:45. There are nine microphones set on a cafeteria table, six cameras on tripods out in front and about forty people milling around.

Just after noon Joe walks in with the Jets' owner, Phil Iselin, and the coach, Weeb Ewbank. He is operating briskly, shaking hands with people he hasn't seen for awhile, smiling across the room at some he can't reach. His eyes are flashing the way they do when he hunkers down over center. The time is here and Joe is ready to roll.

Iselin and Ewbank sit down at the table flanking Joe and each gives a short speech suitable to the occasion. Joe says a few words and then the floor is open to questions. The obvious one is first—How much is the new contract worth?

"I don't want to talk about specific figures," Joe says. "But it's better than the old one, I can tell you that. And I'm glad, too. The cost of living has been going up, you know." The famous Namath dimples flash out across the room.

A young reporter over on the left speaks up. "You are an important sports personality," he says. "The fans pay the bills for professional sports. Don't you think they have a right to know how much you are making?"

Joe looks right at the guy. "No," he says.

"You mean to say you don't care about the fans?"

Joe stares at the reporter as though the guy had just sat on a whoopee cushion. "What kind of question is that?" he says. He turns away and then looks back at the guy with half a smile on. "I don't like you already."

Other reporters jump in with questions to fill a yawning vacuum—How are the knees? How do you like the Jets' chances?—and the conference goes on for about half an hour. That feels like about enough and Joe winds up his last answer. "I'd like to end the conference now," he says. "I need to go back and get some rest for the afternoon practice. Just one more thing before we go, however." He's smiling again as he starts to get up. "I want you gentlemen to know that I really *do* care about the fans."

"How about that guy," Joe says later. "Who did he think he was dealing with? Did he think I was going to start stuttering and stammering, 'Uh, no, uh, I mean, I do like the fans, uh…' I don't know what the guy was trying to do."

You seem to handle press conferences and other situations like that pretty well.

"I've had quite a lot of experience at it by now. I came from Alabama to New York and suddenly there were banquets to speak at and television and so on. I wanted to feel comfortable doing those things so I tried to teach myself to handle them."

You seem to turn yourself on whenever something like that comes up.

"Sure. That's a time to be sharp. The cameras go on and you have to perform. I can do it pretty well by now but there was a time when it came harder. I remember the first time I had to do a song-and-dance number for a TV show. I was embarrassed at that. I felt everybody there was looking at me, getting ready to laugh when I blew it. But that's not the way it was. The show business people understood the situation and I didn't. They knew that doing a number like that is work. Getting it to where it plays right is not an easy thing to do for anybody. That's why they have rehearsals for three or four days before they do a show."

It must make you feel pretty good to be able to handle yourself on stage like that.

"I enjoy doing it, most of the time, but basically it's just business. I don't get into a star thing about it. I know who's standing up there doing the talking. It's just Joe Namath from Beaver Falls. Maybe it's time for national television to be watching and I'm opening up an envelope to announce a winner. But it's still only me standing there."

That's right, you were on the Academy Awards show a while ago. How did you like that?

"That was a gas. It was an experience. You know, you're sitting there during rehearsals and here comes Frank Sinatra and he says, 'Joe, how's it going?' 'Pretty good. How you been?' That's fun. I like talking to him. He's Sinatra, he's been around, I appreciate what he's done, and he's a nice guy, we're talking. Or I meet Jimmy Durante, he says, 'How you doing, Joe?' Sammy Davis. Don Rickles. It's fun talking to those people. They're good dudes. But you know being around all those people was funny in a way. It was strange."

How do you mean?

"I still can't quite picture myself in that situation. Here I am on stage with Sinatra over here, Bing Crosby over here and Bob Hope and people all over and I look around and I say, 'What am I doing here? How did this happen?' Sure I've been in a few movies, but the Academy Awards, that's a big thing to those people out there. It really wasn't to me, because I haven't been around that scene much, but I can appreciate it's important because it's important to so many people. They really get excited about it and I'm happy for them. But here I am in this big thing and all I can think is 'Why? How did I get here?' "

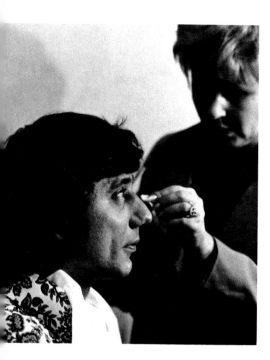

That must have made it pretty hard to handle yourself on camera if things like that were going through your head.

"No, I'm talking about rehearsals. When it got down to the time when the cameras were on, it was all, 'Ladies and Gentlemen, It Gives Me Great Pleasure ...' You know, you do your thing then. But at rehearsals it was weird. I'd be up there on stage and I'd look out into the audience and I'd see my lawyer, Jimmy Walsh. Now I can relate to Jimmy, he's my buddy, we know each other. And we just enjoyed what was happening. That whole trip, man, that was a gas. Just watching, just learning, digging the people, digging the situation."

Learning, you say. What is there to learn from a situation like that?

"Well, people for instance. How do people handle themselves? Sometimes they go through some strange changes. Like, I'm sitting here talking to this lady, an actress, and we're just talking along and some guy comes up to her and says, 'You're on in ten minutes,' and Bang! that lady just changed her whole thing. She straightened up and her face pulled together and her voice changed. I mean, she went 'on' right then. She's an actress, you know, a professional. I guess that's how she relates lots of times."

You say you didn't really feel you belonged with people like that. But as far as being a big name in the country, you could be as big as anybody you saw.

"Possibly, depending on how you look at it. Jimmy Walsh showed me something a while ago that I got a big kick out of. It was in one of the newspaper columns and whether it was right or wrong, it was fun. There was a poll of the children down at the Republican Convention a year ago asking them for their favorites. They got the results and the name that got the most votes was Flipper. Then came President Nixon. Third was Joe Namath. I got a kick out of that. I told Jimmy I don't mind being third in that company."

But things like that don't make you feel you belong on stage with big stars?

"Well, I understand it. I can think it through and see where it adds up. But it still feels strange."

You don't have that big an ego?

"I was the fourth son in my family, you know. A fourth son doesn't get much chance to feel big-headed because every time he starts to, he gets himself slapped down. So I was kind of used to watching my head, and when I got to New York maybe I was careful to try not to get too big an ego. I stress not feeling like that because it would make me feel bad that I would have that kind of opinion of myself. And I had some help, too. I heard about it and heard about it and heard about it. I'd read in the newspapers where I was supposed to have a big head and guys would come up to me in bars, guys who I never met before, and tell me what a conceited jerk I was. Maybe those people didn't know me, and maybe what they said wasn't right, but it helped me keep track of myself.''

Wasn't it a temptation to get into the big-name New York night life?

''No, for a simple reason. A lot of the things I got to do because of my name, I liked what I was doing before a little better anyway. Rather than going out to a banquet or party, I'd just clown around with some friends—dinner, dancing, movies, stuff like that. A lot of that stuff, the parties and big dinners and things like that make me feel uncomfortable. They're just too crowded. So I had to look at the situation and say, 'Why am I out here at this banquet, or whatever, if I'd rather be home?' Well, it was business, see, it was a good thing commercially. So I started looking at business as business, and kept my life away from business.''

Wait a minute. What is it you are calling business here?

''Something like going to the Academy Awards with all kinds of photographers around and walking in with a beautiful lady on your arm.''

That's business?

''Sure it is. When we got invited to do that thing, I wasn't even sure I wanted to go, but Jimmy thought it would be good from the overall business aspect, public exposure and so on, and so we went. But that was business. I'm not walking in there with Raquel Welch and saying, ''Look at me! Aren't I great!' No. This is work. This is a job I'm doing for this day. And the man

doing it is still Joe Namath from Beaver Falls.

Joe Namath from Beaver Falls. It occurred to me after we played catch a while ago that most guys in the country would probably rather play catch with Joe Namath than shake hands with the President.

"I hope so. It sounds like more fun to me, playing catch. I hope people are still into having a good time."

We arrive at his building in a limousine. He has an apartment in the East 80s off Fifth Avenue on a block with lovely old buildings and an air of tranquility rare in New York City. At the end of the shady street, just across Fifth, the columns of the Metropolitan Museum of Art shine in the sun.

We go in a doorway etched in iron scroll-work and up one flight of red-carpeted stairs to his door. He turns keys in both locks, and Joe Namath is home. Just inside, all shiny wood and stuffed leather with a mirrored cabinet behind, is the first conversation piece—a small but entirely adequate bar.

This is a new apartment for Joe. A couple of years ago he left his first one, the one he shared with several friends and carpeted in four inches of shaggy white, and now he lives alone in two big floors of elegant, bygone opulence.

There are three rooms on the first floor. Just to the left, off the foyer-bar, is the living room, a large room furnished in comfortable rococo. To the right, with a marvelous bay window stretching up to the high ceiling and cherubic angels carved above

Arriving at the Academy Awards with Raquel Welch is all in a business day

the door, is the game room. This room is dominated by a heavily carved pool table set in at a diagonal. In one corner is an automatic "bowling" machine, in another a slot machine, and high up against a wall, suspended from the ceiling in a golden chain, is a color television set. You never have to move much to watch Monday night football at Joe's place because he has one of these air-borne TV rigs in each major room. He also has thirteen telephone extensions, which seems slightly less excessive after watching what Joe goes through whenever he has to stand up.

At the rear of the first floor is a brightly decorated kitchen and dining area but it is not until he leads the way upstairs, up a four-tiered switchback stairway that the apartment attains its focal point. On this floor are a small guest room, a good-sized bathroom and the master bedroom.

Done in golds and browns, soft and rich, Joe's room is so huge it manages to dwarf a bed which must be advertised as emperor size. Opposite the bed there is an ornate fireplace set in a wall that is mostly mirror and the mirrors continue up and all the way across the ceiling. The wall behind the bed is curtained, and two antique wall lamps curve their way out and over the head of the bed.

In a room full of plants, small statues and brass fixtures from the Middle East, the dominant attraction is a massive Tiffany floor lamp with a flowing metal base and pole and a radiant shade of multi-colored glass. As we enter the darkened room, soft reds and blues and golds from this lamp float through the air.

Joe flips on some lights. "It's a nice place, don't you think?" he asks. "Too bad there's no place in New York where you can have some space and be comfortable." He flops down on the enormous bed, rolls over to his left, and hits a button on the wall. Rock music comes booming out of two big speakers near the ceiling in the corners opposite the bed.

"And look at this," he says, rolling over to the opposite edge and sitting up so he can open a closet door. Inside the closet is a refrigerator. Inside the refrigerator is some champagne. "I'm not really crazy about champagne," he says, "but it's nice to have around just in case someone likes it."

The visitors, male and female, who come to this apartment with a notion of how the legend ought to look are not disappointed. Joe Namath knows how Joe Namath is supposed to live.

Today's guest falls back into a La-Z-Boy reclining chair near the fireplace. Either from integrity or convenience, Joe really does use the products he endorses—the reclining chair, Puma shoes, the Hamilton Beach popcorn popper. For awhile we

Shooting pool with friends in the comfort of home

just hang out with Jose Feliciano coming from the speakers and Alabama beating somebody on the TV. Watching his old school do it right makes Joe happy, but he can't see the whole game. As on most every other day of his autumn life, he has some business to attend to. A film crew is coming over to do an interview.

There's a buzz at the door in about half an hour and Joe goes to answer.

"Hey, Joe," comes a loud voice. "How you doing, Joe?" There are three guys there and it looks like they have enough equipment stacked up in the hall to film a football game.

"This is Rickie, Joe," the loud one goes on, "this is Jeff, and I'm Burt. Nice of you to let us come over here and shoot you. It'll only take about a half hour to do, you know, like we said. We don't want to hang you up."

It takes them half an hour just to set up the equipment, and that's with most of it left outside. They decide to shoot in the game room, to interview Joe while he's playing pool.

What with equipment problems, retakes and extra camera angles, the session is heading toward its third hour before the interview is completed. After dismantling their equipment, all three of the guys follow Namath into his kitchen.

"Hey, Joe," the lead guy says. "Did Jimmy tell you about the other plan? You know, what we want to do is we want to make you a movie that you'll be able to keep and be proud of after you've retired. You know? We want to follow you around all next year and film you every place and

then make a one hour TV film out of it. It'll look nice on TV but the thing you ought to think about is that it's a film you'll be able to keep and look back at in years to come. It's really for your benefit."

The guy is a little pushy, the kind who'd have his hand clapped on Namath's shoulder if he had the nerve. Joe is standing over the sink, washing up some dishes.

"I don't know," Joe says. "I don't think I'd want to put in all that work."

"Oh, hey," the film guy says. "It won't be that much work. We'll just do a little shooting now and then."

"You just said you wanted to follow me around everywhere all year."

"Well, I mean. It doesn't take much time to shoot, you know. We won't take up much of your time."

"Yeah. This interview was only supposed to take a half hour, too." Joe is walking toward the door now with the film crew following along. "Maybe we can talk about it next spring some time."

"Sure. OK. Sure, Joe. We'll talk to you next spring."

Joe holds the door open and the three guys shake hands with him and step out.

"Don't forget," the one guy says as Joe starts to close the

door. "It would be a great thing to have after you retire."

"Sometimes it's like that," Joe says. "I don't want to hurt anybody's feelings, but I have to live my life, too. I can't give my time to all the people that want some or do every project that anybody wants to do."

How do you keep from getting hemmed in?

"Basically, that's Jimmy Walsh's part of the job. He handles most of the business dealings and if he and I agree on a project after he has set it up, then we roll. I'm willing to work when it's time to work and the deal is all settled before hand. But otherwise, boy, my time is my own. I enjoy just leisure living."

So you keep your celebrity status from hanging you up too much.

"Yeah. And it's like the traveling. There are some restrictions I feel from being a star or something, but most of the restrictions I do feel, the things I've had to avoid, for the most part I believe they have been beneficial to me."

How do you mean?

"Take things like drinking and maybe drinking too much, or driving while I'm drunk or driving too fast, or you know, little things like littering the streets. I've tried to avoid stuff like that. I just think how it looks if somebody I get a big charge out of on the athletic field or on a movie screen does something on the street, in real life, that turns me off. To me, that's a down. It gives me a bad taste. I've seen a few people in show business act a little crazy when they drink and really humiliate people, really be nasty to them. And since I've been in pro ball, I've become more conscious of how I am with people, how I come on to people, and I think it's helped me in the long run."

Did you ever do something in public that you really regretted?

"Boy, I did. I mentioned this briefly in my first book, but it was really important to me. It happened at an airport. I was with a lady, and I was late for a business thing and my plane was delayed one hour in one town and two hours in another town and I was a little uptight about it. My nerves were in trouble. We went to get a bite to eat while we were stuck on the ground and while we were walking to the restaurant we ran into a troop of boy scouts. Okay. Visit with the boys and sign autographs. That's all right. We got through that and finally got in to eat. We ordered and the food came and just then this guy walked up to the table. He was a little drunk. I've just picked up my knife and fork and he comes up and says, 'Hi, Joe. Sign this. You don't mind, do you?' I was really ticked by this time. I said, 'Hell yes, I do. I'm eating.' The guy straightened up real quick and said 'I'm sorry,' and went outside. I watched him leave and outside was his wife, I assume, and another couple, and this guy had to walk up to them with a hang dog look on his face. He was really embarrassed. And I felt so bad that I made this guy feel bad. You know, a minute ago he was a happy, jovial guy. Now he was feeling terrible. It ruined my

whole meal. I must have thought about it fifty times after that — a hundred times. And every time I did, I felt bad. If I make somebody else feel bad, I feel bad, and I really learned from that time. I don't have to experience that feeling if I understand myself more, if I cool out some, be more relaxed and control my nerves. So I'm sorry about that guy, and if I've ever hurt anybody else, but I don't think of this as a restriction. I think it has helped me, helped me learn about myself."

It's a Wednesday or Thursday about a month into training camp. Joe's arm is tired and his passes have been looking ill for about ten days and his mood has been darkening steadily.

He's not saying much as we come down the elevator of the main-floor dormitory at Hofstra University, the Jets' training camp, and head out the door for the walk to lunch. As Joe appears, fifteen or twenty kids swarm around him, shouting for his autograph. Usually he handles this scene well, signing as he walks along talking to the kids. About a week earlier he had come down with a beer in his hand and then stopped at the door. "Whoops," he said, "there's kids out there." He stuffed the bottle in the front of his pants and pulled his sweatshirt down over the bulge, and with the bad example tucked safely away, he had signed and joked until all the kids were satisfied. But he didn't forget the beer. In the privacy of his car he took it out as we drove away.

It's more fun talking to folks, anyway.

Today, however, there is nothing light-hearted about him. Grabbing a pen, he signs his name quickly, almost angrily, as he strides along, then says, "Don't walk in front of me, boys." But they do, and he trips a little on one of them. "Get out from in front of me, would you," he says. It's a grumpy scene.

When the cloud of kids has finally dissipated, we move into the student union. In the lunch room I set up a tape mike in an ash tray and try to get him interested in talking about how to beat the "Double-Double" pass defense, but I find myself doing most of the talking. Something reminds me of the team I grew up with, the Los Angeles Rams, and he asks if they ever won a championship. "Once," I tell him, "in 1951, when they had a great passing attack. That was when they had Bob Waterfield and Norm Van Brocklin and Tom Fears and Elroy Hirsch."

"And single coverage," Joe says. "One man covering one pass receiver. What ever happened to single coverage?"

He puts up a flickering half-smile and keeps working on his food. I turn off the recorder and we finish eating in silence. The rest of the team has already left and when Joe finally pushes his dishes away there is nobody else in the room. He has his head down and his forearms are resting on the table top. Suddenly he pounds the table with both fists. "Damn!" He's nearly hollering. "Damn, boy!"

"What's the matter," I ask him.

He turns away in his chair a little. "I haven't got my trip together at *all*," he says.

"What trip?"

"Football," he says, turning back to stare at me. "Football. I'm not setting up right, I'm not throwing right. I've got nothing going out there at all."

He puts his head down again and waits a little. Then he says, "It's going to be different today, though. Today I'm going to…" His voice trails away and he looks out the window at deep gray clouds and trees blowing in the wind.

"C'mon, *rain*," he says.

"Football can be tough on you," Joe says later. "It can be a humbling experience. More than humbling—downright humiliating. It'll keep your head in line, buddy."

You are one of the game's stars. Has it been humiliating to you?

"I'll tell you it's been. I've had six of my passes intercepted in one half. In one *half*. You're trying to keep your confidence up and here come six guys running your passes back at you. We get some nice things done out there, and it feels good to do it right, but there's not much chance to get an inflated opinion of yourself. You have to learn respect for the other guy because you may beat him on this play, but he's a pro, boy, and he's going to turn around and beat you on the next one. You learn how to be a gracious winner and an understanding loser. I appreciate what the game has done for my head that way."

In terms of winning and losing?

"Yeah, that, and also it does good things for being honest. I'm a pretty confident guy. I know what my abilities are. I know that if you add up all the things a quarterback needs— the ability to throw, to read defenses, to call plays, to lead the team—that nobody has ever played the position any better than I do. But there's no way I can try to say I'm the son of superman. I find out differently every Sunday.

"Sometimes I've thrown a lousy pass and one of my guys just happens to get there and catch the ball and the play turns into something nice. People come into the locker room afterward and they're telling me, 'Great pass. Way to throw.' I can't take that. It's not a good feeling."

What do you do about it?

"I've got to let somebody know it was luck, that it just turned out that way. I'm a religious guy, too, and that has something to do with this. I don't mean I'm religious like some people where they are steady church goers and they don't cuss and so on, but as far as believing in God and that he is responsible for everything, I'm a firm believer in that. I was raised in a religious background and I went to Catholic school and a firm idea of God has just always been with me as far back as I can remember. He's there and he knows and the thing is I know I can't cheat him. I can't get big-headed about anything because if I do I get embarrassed about it."

Thinking that way ought to keep your pride down.

"Yeah, it helps. You know, the basics of life are really pretty simple, at least the basics of *my* life. I was being interviewed for television last year and they asked me what I take pride in. I didn't want to talk about it on national television because I could just hear people saying, 'Who is this kid, talking like that?' But really all I want to do is enjoy myself some and try to treat other people the way I want my family and myself treated."

Isn't it hard to be a celebrity and still treat people well all the time?

"I think it's easier for me than most people. I'm sure it would be tougher on me to try to be nice to people if I worked a six-day week and took home $500 a month."

What specifics are you thinking of?

"I don't want to be cheated, say. I wouldn't want my wife to go out with anybody else, and I don't want to take out anybody's wife. It's not right, and it's so simple to do things right, not to cheat or to lie, not to be rude to somebody and hurt them. Your mind isn't troubled five minutes later, ten minutes later, years later. You don't have to look back and say, 'How could I do that?' We're all in this thing together, you know, all the people, all the animals even, and the plants, too. It's got to be easier on the mind if we don't deliberately give each other trouble."

Humiliation is your defense going onto the field because of an interception

Talking on one of the two phones in the kitchen of the Manhattan apartment

You think we should be kind to plants?

"Yeah, I like them. I talk to trees occasionally, you know, like, 'Hey, how you doing.' They're a part of life and I am a part of life. Maybe it doesn't seem like they're communicating with me, but at least I can try to communicate with them and let them know I'm on their side, that we're friends. The other day when I was outside, I saw a flower. It was just a little flower, a pretty one, and I started to go over and pick it. But then I said no, why do that? You ever feel that way? I just figured that flower didn't want to be broken off and killed. It was probably ridiculous, but I didn't think that was the right thing to do to that flower."

There is some evidence that plants have feelings.

"It makes sense to me. You know, I've got a lot of plants in my bedroom. I wonder how they feel about being in there?"

They certainly look healthy.

"That's true. They look good. They must be feeling all right."

Joe opens up his refrigerator and pulls out a carton of plain yogurt. He eats a lot of yogurt and also the kind of quick breakfast drink you mix with milk. A late evening dinner is usually his only solid meal of the day.

"What are you weighing now?" I ask him.

"I've lost those three or four pounds," he says. "I'm down around 203, 204. You know what that extra weight was? It was the good life at training camp — three meals a day, regular hours." He heads out toward the living room, yogurt in hand. "I should have known living right ain't good for me."

Joe sets his yogurt down on the floor by a chair in the living room and goes into an alcove to pull out his movie projector and two cans of film. As he carries the stuff back into the living room he says, "We've got the Colts this week. They play some pass defense on that team I'll tell you that. They make you work a day." Joe has a way sometimes of hunching up his shoulders as he walks, looking out the corner of his eye with a little grin and then giving out with a high-pitched know-it-all chuckle. Thinking about the Colts has got him doing it now.

"What are you laughing at if they're so good?"

He puts on the falsetto chuckle again. "We're going to make them work a day, too, boy," he says. He's still smiling as he threads the projector and gets ready to flash the Baltimore defense on a small angled wall in one corner of the room. Like most quarterbacks Joe spends a lot of time at home watching movies of his team's opponents. He has to keep current on their latest strategy and pick up on the personal characteristics of each of the eleven ballplayers executing that strategy. Even with seven years of experience, there is no way to get beyond this nightly homework. In football, things are always changing.

Joe watches the shifting patterns quietly, intently, com-

menting only now and then. "They're rolling the zone up top in this situation," he says. "We can take a quick out down here right away." He punches the action back and forth with a small switch in his left hand, back and forth, back and forth, combing the screen for the details, the "keys," that will unlock the Colt defense on Sunday.

Suddenly the machine goes off altogether. Namath rolls his head back and looks at the ceiling.

"Oh, man!" he says. "I just thought of something. Look at this." He turns the projector on again and runs the last play back.

"Look how they're playing against the slot formation."

In the film the Colts are meeting the New England Patriots and on this play the Patriots have lined up in a slot formation with both of their fast wide receivers on the right and only the tight end on the left.

"You see that." Joe says. "The Colts are putting three backs over on those two wide receivers. That leaves only one guy to cover the tight end." Most tight ends are not too fast but the tight end on the Jets is Richard Caster. Caster is one of the swiftest men in the game.

"If they only put one man on Richard," Joe says, "he can just blow right by the guy. We can go deep on them right now."

Joe gets up quickly and heads for the kitchen. While he has been watching the film, he has forgotten about the carton of yogurt that is still on the floor and he kicks it getting up. It blotches out all over the carpet. "Nice going, Joe," he says, and makes the trip to the kitchen a short one, returning immediately with paper towels. With deft motions he surrounds the mess and plucks it up. A couple of light wipes and there are no traces left.

"You're pretty good at that," I tell him.

"I should be," he says. "I spill a lot of things."

For whatever reason, Joe is a good housekeeper. He folds the projector up and puts it away the minute he is done with it, even though he uses it every night, and that is typical of his behavior in the apartment.

Out at training camp, living in a college dorm with sixty other football players, Joe keeps his room about the way a college sophomore does. Clothes and papers are scattered around and the desk is overrun with fan letters, hand-made cards, polaroid snapshots of total strangers and other fall-out from superstar status.

But at home in Manhattan Joe becomes a meticulous housekeeper. He has created a classy environment and he pays the dues the place demands—crawling across the two-acre bed dragging sheets and blankets behind, policing his living room and play room for dirty glasses and ash trays, leaning in over his sink to make sure a small pile of dirty dishes doesn't become a large one. When the maid comes in twice a week she starts with a place that is at least orderly. Joe is a daily host, to friends and sometimes to business acquaintances, and all his visitors find him in an impressive place properly cared for.

Doing the dishes every day might seem to be a trivial virtue, but in Namath's case a clean kitchen points beyond itself to a general way of handling his life: Joe takes care of business.

"My attitude is a simple one," he says, "talking about football, business, whatever. I try to do what I am designated to do to the best of my ability. That way I don't have any puzzles in my head. I don't want to look back on something and say, 'Damn, I think I could have done that better.' When I look back I want to be able to say, 'I tried like hell, boy. I did the best I could.'"

Do you keep this up all the time, or do you let things slide now and then?

"Now and then something gets away, and it hurts every time, too. I'll tell you the last time it happened on something big was in that Baltimore game, the one where Caster caught those two long touchdowns in the fourth quarter. That might have looked like a big game for us—we got six touchdown passes and 496 yards passing and we got those two to Caster at the end based on what we had seen in the films. But it will be a long time before I forget how I felt before the game. That

was a bad feeling. When I woke up that morning I was ticked at myself. I was really upset. I hadn't done the work I should have and I didn't know the game plan well enough at all. Some things had gone on late in the week and I was having a pretty good time and just didn't get around to studying like I should have. And I was lying in that Baltimore hotel room feeling terrible, feeling like I was going to let down forty or fifty guys."

You must have felt better after the game.

"No, man. That was as bad as I've felt after winning a game. We hit some big plays and managed to win, but I couldn't be happy about myself at all. I made more mistakes than I should have, calling the wrong play into the defense, and just generally I wasn't sharp. You talk about disgusted. I came out of the game, took off my helmet and put it in the locker, and went in and sat down in the coach's office. I wanted to talk to somebody that could understand."

Who did you talk to?

"Kenny Meyer, the offensive coach. I just wasn't ready to talk to newspapermen or anybody except a coach. My emotions were so mixed. I was so down about the way I played I didn't know how to approach it with the press. So we talked about the things that had happened in the game, the things that went wrong, and then I asked him what I should tell the press. He said, 'Just tell them we played poorly and got lucky. Sometimes we play well and lose.'"

Did talking to Meyer help?

"Some, yeah. But that was

still a bad feeling. That's why I try to do my work as well as I can. There was never a time the rest of the season where I felt I hadn't prepared enough. I didn't want to be in that place again."

Quarterback is a demanding job. Is there anything to do that will lighten the load of responsibility?

"The best thing I know is just to know your job and get control of it. Have complete confidence in what you're doing."

How do you know if you have complete confidence?

"If you're not afraid to gamble in any situation. If you can go ahead and throw for six points any time you see an opening. Talking about gambling over in Las Vegas, say, I like to do that some but I'm still a percentage man and I know the percentages are against me there even before I start. But out on the field I have to have the feeling I can call what I see any time. And I know what it feels like not to have that confidence. When I came back from my knee injury against San Francisco, I wasn't completely confident. And I had good reason not to be confident. I'd only been practicing a week or something and I knew I wasn't as sharp as I should be. Even if you are the best at something, still you have to be *at* your best in a game as tough as pro football. When I went out on that field, I wasn't feeling too awfully good."

Had you ever been that nervous before?

"Not often playing football. I learned where that kind of nervousness comes from once when I was playing golf. I was playing a golf exhibition with Paul Bryant, my coach down at Alabama. There were 10,000 people there watching, and I'll tell you I was really upset. We walked down the fairway from the first tee and I told Paul, 'This is awful. I was so nervous back there I couldn't even take the club back. I've never been this nervous.' And Bryant said, 'There's a bunch of people watching you do something you don't have that much confidence in. This isn't football, where you've worked so hard for so long to prepare yourself.' And when he said that, it sunk in. That's how I get confidence in my play. I prepare myself before-hand until I know that I can do what I have to. Then I have faith."

Do you think of yourself as a hard worker?

"I know some guys work harder. They feel the load is so heavy they should study all the time. But as long as I'm satisfied I have my work done right, I can't see eating and drinking and sleeping it. Of course, I find myself thinking about it a lot, calling plays in situations. Sometimes I'll be shooting a game of pool and I'll find myself calling plays against a 5-1 No Exchange. But once I know what's happening, I don't keep studying and studying. It's best for me to relax, to have some fun and keep the tension from

Talking to Bubba Smith in Baltimore

building up. That's how I perform best."

Have you ever done any weight-lifting to strengthen your arm?

"The only time I ever lifted weights in my life, I pulled a muscle. I had been lifting for about two weeks and we were out at practice and I went up to catch a pass and damn if I didn't pull a muscle up under my right shoulder blade. I haven't ever lifted weights since. I've thought about it some. In fact, I give it a lot of thought, but I just don't ever get around to doing it. And I'm not sure that's bad. I'm pretty happy with the way things are going and maybe I shouldn't take a chance again."

What's the hardest job you have to do?

"Well, usually I don't do anything hard. A hard job for me is a job I don't like doing, and Jimmy Walsh and I try to keep that kind from coming up. I don't mind working if I like what I'm doing—playing football or doing this book or doing a movie. The way I look at it, the hardest thing isn't a job. The hardest thing is just taking care of yourself, doing the right thing about eating and sleeping and taking care of your body. I think that's hard for everybody. There's always something more you could be doing for yourself and if you don't do it, boy, that's one thing nobody else is going to do for you. You don't have a mother all your life."

Speaking of mothers, how's yours?

"She's fine. She's great. I call her all the time on the phone and she always wants to know how I'm doing, if I'm taking care of myself. She's quite some lady. Did I tell you the story about her and the Buffalo police?"

No, go ahead.

"A lot of my family went up to the Buffalo game one year, my mother and stepfather and two of my brothers and several nieces and nephews. After we got back to New York, I called mom up to see if they got home all right, and she says, 'Oh, honey, three rahs for the Buffalo police.' Then she told me what happened. After the game, they were stranded at the stadium when the bus left early, so they started walking, but it's a residential district and no cabs were going by. Finally my brothers went to phone for one, leaving my mother with all the kids and my stepfather, who doesn't speak too much English. They kept looking down the street when here comes a paddy wagon. Mom doesn't worry about that. She runs out into the street, flags down the paddy wagon and tells the policemen her troubles. They're feeling good and invite the whole crew to hop in. By now, my brothers are a half mile down the street. When the paddy wagon pulls up to them, my stepfather is looking out the back and my brothers are thinking, 'Oh, no, what did he do?' Then my mother jumps out and they like to die. But there was no reason to worry—the police had room for two more. My mom is big in Buffalo."

Do you get along with her well?

"Yeah, the way the two of us relate is really great. All these things have gone on in my life, but for her nothing has changed. I'm still her boy. 'Don't put your hands in your pockets, Joe. Don't walk with your head down, Joe.' "

Doesn't it bother you to have her still talking like that?

"No, it's great. I still *am* the same guy she always knew. She's probably the one person who really knows me well, who understands me."

Maybe we should talk to her some for the book.

"No, don't bother. Mothers don't understand."

Joe is hungry and he's digging around in two immense closets for something to wear when he goes out. It's about 11 o'clock at night and jeans aren't appropriate now. After a little rummaging, he settles on dark slacks and a white pullover sweater. He stands facing the fireplace wall, the mirrored wall, pulls his sweater down and reaches up to mess his hair into place. He has the kind of hair that if he keeps it shaggy cut just right, he never has to pay it much attention. He used to get a lot of static about his hair, of course, but the only time he hears about it now is when he gets it cut too short and his teammates jump on him.

A couple of his friends have come over, which is usual, and everybody is going out for a late dinner at "the club," Bachelors III, the restaurant and bar that caused the front page commotion with NFL Commissioner Pete Rozelle in 1969. Joe sold his interest in the New York club to appease Rozelle, although he still has interests in other restaurants around the country. I asked him once what he thinks of Rozelle now. "I don't," he said. "I don't think about him."

We go downstairs and Joe hustles across Fifth Avenue with his trademark trot—leaning forward, legs stiff, feet trailing out behind—and he catches a cab to take us on the twenty-block ride to the club. "I haven't had a square meal in two days," he says. "I'm ready for this."

Bachelors III has recently been remodeled in red plush and white stucco with dark brown beams and original paintings on each wall. The largest painting is of Joe Namath, No. 12, in green and white and grim visage. If the place is being frequented by any undesirable types these days, they are cleverly disguised as pretty East Side females and visiting bankers from Ohio.

We take up a position at the near end of the bar, which turns out to be a staging area for a later foray to the back, and stay there long enough for a leisurely drink and some pleasant conversation. A number of people come up to Joe and it soon becomes obvious that a night on the town with Namath is something other than an endless search for cheap thrills. He likes to spend some time out drinking with his friends because that's where he feels comfortable. He is from a small town in Pennsylvania by way of four college years in another small place, Tuscaloosa, Alabama, and the late night life in a comfortable club has a lot in common with the feel of small towns.

It's a natural place for Namath, because he's a friendly man. He likes to meet people and talk and laugh with them. These are things no one can do very well elsewhere in the public places of New York City, least of all Namath, who has to be constantly on the watch for hustlers and operators. But in the small community of a club, where people are well known and life is laid back, he can relax and come out. Liquor in manageable amounts has some advantages, but the comfortable, friendly life in these small nighttime communities is the real attraction.

As he sits at the bar several conversations succeed one another, wives and girl friends are introduced, and Joe is friendly, courteous and enjoying himself. He has a gift for making people feel comfortable and he acts with an unfeigned sense of good manners inculcated by his mother back home and enhanced by four years in the South.

A young guy comes up and says, "I just wanted to say hi, Mr. Namath." They shake hands and a few sentences are exchanged, then the guy says, "I'm sure glad to see you playing again. I hope you don't mind but I've always wanted to ask you this. Why did you try to make that tackle against Detroit in 1971?"

August, 1971: Paul Naumoff rolls off and Mike Lucci (53) rolls on as Joe grabs for the injured left knee that would keep him out until November

He's talking about the pre-season play that tore up Joe's left knee. Joe fixes a small smile on his face, looks up at a corner of the room for a minute and then looks back at the guy. "Now, I don't want to seem like I'm being wise or anything," he says, "but that's a dumb question. A lot of people have asked it, but it's still a dumb question. Did you ever play any football?" The guy shakes his head slightly. "When you're out there on the field, there's a game going on. If some guy is trying to run past you and score a touchdown, you tackle him, that's all." Joe takes a sip of his drink, waiting for a rebuttal that doesn't come, then asks, "As a football player, how would you feel if one of your teammates stood there and watched some guy go by with the ball? I know how I'd feel. I'd tell the dumb sucker to get the hell off the field if he didn't want to play. A player has to have self-respect. It's not only the guys on your team you're thinking about but also your family and the people you know. If you put the uniform on, you're supposed to be a football player."

He isn't trying to make the guy feel bad but this is a topic that bothers him and by now there are five or six people listening in. After a moment of quiet, Joe thinks of a story that will lighten the mood some.

"It's like Paul Bryant used to tell us," he says. "You know Bryant, the coach down at Alabama?" The guy nods. "One time at Texas A & M Coach Bryant was talking to the team in the locker room before the game.

'Now, damn!' he says. 'Y'all going to run all over this team here. This team can't beat you. They're not *supposed* to beat you. They ain't got families near as good as your families. Their mommas and daddies ain't near as good as your mommas and daddies. Y'all just a better class of folks than they are. Now y'all ain't going to go out there and let your folks down, are you?'

"When Coach Bryant got through with his speech, the Aggies ran out and beat that team something awful. It was really bad. After the game the TV guys came in and they got a couple of the heroes for that day and put them up on the stand and the announcer asked one of the guys, 'Why did you do so well out there today?' He stuck the microphone in the player's face and the guy said, 'Because we got better mommas and daddies than they do.' "

There's a good laugh all around and Joe smiles and tells the young guy, "That was a little strange, you know, but that's what I'm talking about. You don't want to let people down when you're out there on the field."

Things are smoothed and pretty soon the guy goes back to his table. As he leaves, Jimmy Walsh walks up. Jimmy is Namath's long-time friend from the University of Alabama. He is also Namath's lawyer. He is a smallish, red-haired, slightly rounding man with a twinkle in his eye and an angle on his mind. He is the kind of man you could work with for years based on nothing more than his word. Joe Namath has his legal flank comfortably covered.

Jimmy has come out to tell Joe what the situation is in back. There are several business people there, people Joe has endorsement contracts with, and Jimmy has brought them over to have dinner and to spend a little time with Joe. Joe nods and we all go back to a table next to Walsh's. He sits with Jimmy's group for awhile, laughing and talking and telling how his legs are. It's a painless way to do business. It's another reason to come out to the club.

When Joe returns to our table we are joined by a pretty blonde I've seen Joe with before. By the time we have all had dinner and a couple of nightcaps it is closing in on 4 o'clock. That's 4 A.M. Namath lives his life about four hours later than most of us: for him 7 o'clock in the morning comes at about 11 and midnight arrives at 4 A.M. It is a schedule dictated by two main considerations. The Jets start their meeting at noon and in New York the bars close at 4.

Finally, in no hurry, we all move toward the door. A couple of us grab cabs. Joe and his lady get into a limousine for the short ride home.

Nobody will be getting up too early in the morning but then, in a group of athletes, dancers, actors, restauranteurs and free-lance writers, nobody has to.

"I like the restaurant business," Joe says. "That's a good way to enjoy life. I like to meet people and talk. In the restaurant business you make money, meet people and give them something better than what they've got. You are giving them a nice place to spend an evening, a nice atmosphere with good food."

Is this something you would like to do after you retire from football?

"Sure. I like it now. People ask me sometimes what would happen if I lost all my money now that I've had some. But I never spend any time thinking about that. I know I can earn a living. I'd work. I've always worked, although my brothers probably wouldn't agree with that. If I had to work I could coach a football team, for one thing. Television's been pretty good for me, too, and I've had some experience in movies. And there's the restaurant business. If I was flat broke and out, I'd get a job and get a little capital together and go into the restaurant business again. But the thing is, I don't think about things like that. I don't worry about the future. If I do the jobs well that I have now, then I've got my security taken care of, so I don't have to think about the years ahead. Do you know what you're going to be doing ten years from now? I don't. I don't have any idea."

And that doesn't bother you?

"Why should it bother me? Life's going on and interesting

A candid camera scene shot from Joe's limousine—moving on New York streets

things keep happening and I just roll with it and try to get into whatever's going on. Ten years ago I sure didn't think I'd be doing what I'm doing now. When I was back in Beaver Falls as a kid I didn't have any idea what I was going to do. All I knew was I wanted out of there."

You didn't like the town?

"The town's fine. There's a lot of nice people there, but what is there to do for a living in Beaver Falls? My father worked in the steel mills. Should I be doing that? I had a couple of summer jobs when I was in high school working for the city, for the recreation department. I remember one time I somehow had a job scraping a swimming pool. It was the hottest part of town in the middle of a hot summer and I'm in the bottom of this pit scraping off paint. With a four-inch scraper. Now that was a job I didn't do as well as it could have been done. I didn't do that one too fast. And after a few jobs like that, I decided to join the Air Force. I wasn't going to get caught in the steel mills— or anybody else's swimming pool, unless it was full of water."

Why the Air Force?

"I wanted to fly a plane. I think I could be a good pilot if I studied and applied myself. My brother John was in the army for a career and he got a pretty good education touring the world, going to Europe and the Far East. I figured I'd try that. Anything to get out of the life of a damn eight-to-four job."

What is it you don't like about that?

"The monotony. The drag, the same old routine every day. I can't stand running the same trip all the time. I looked around Beaver Falls and I'd think about myself being thirty years old in that town with a wife and how many children. Maybe I'd have had ten years in the mill by then and I'd get up in the morning and say, 'What am I going to do today? Back to the mill. What am I going to do next year? Back to the mill. Ten years from now? The same thing.' And what could I give my family? Just a basic upbringing. I appreciated that myself. I appreciated the way my father worked for us. But there's no reason I had to do that, too."

The restaurant business is different?

"To me it is. There's no routine and the work I do is mainly dealing with people, which I like. It's a nice way to work, dealing with people. I like the same thing about football, dealing with people, working together. To me this is the best part of the game, the association with the guys on the team."

Vince Lombardi used to say the players on a football team have to love one another.

"I don't know if love is the right word, but the idea is good. You're in there fighting together, and you look out for each other. You take care of each other. But I don't know if that means you love each other. It depends on how you generally use the word. I don't usually say that I *love* John Riggins."

You are known for having a few lady friends, however.

"Yeah, I enjoy women. There are some ladies that have been pretty good to me. I appreciate them."

What about the people who think it's a disgrace the way you carry on?

"I can't figure that out. It seems to me it would be un-American if a healthy bachelor didn't like to take women out to dinner now and then, have a nice time. It's just a natural feeling. I can't say I spend time worrying about people who think it isn't natural."

Do you ever get the urge to settle down, pick one lady and stay with her?

"I have had that feeling a couple of times in the past. I've been in situations with women, a couple of girls that I guess you'd say I was really in love with. But that's the wrong thing for me at this point in time. I'm just not ready to settle down. I still like to travel, see new places, have new experiences, and I'm still working toward the security I want for my family. And one other thing, when I'm in love and away from my girl, that is a bad feeling. It's a bad, sick feeling, standing in a hotel room and looking out the window and missing somebody that you love that's thousands of miles away. I decided I didn't want to have that feeling anymore. And it's for the best right now. As long as I'm into moving, a

lady and I would just be giving each other a bunch of trouble by trying to have a permanent relationship. I'm just not into the final part yet. Marriage. I just don't have the urge to partake."

You are staying free. Does it bother you if a lady you are seeing is also free and seeing someone else?

"It shouldn't, I know that. And in a way it's better because then we're not leaning on each other. But really, I don't want to know about it. There's a part of me that it bothers, so it's fine just so I don't have to hear about it."

It sounds like the relationship with football players would be simpler and easier to handle.

"It's different, but I'm not sure it's easier. A team feeling is not just a rah-rah, superficial kind of thing. You go through a lot together, working hard and winning some and losing some, and you get pretty tight. And it's not that easy working together. Especially at quarterback it can get to be a problem as far as play calling and leadership go."

How do you mean?

"We'll be out there in the huddle and a receiver will say, 'I can beat this guy,' and somebody else on the line will say, 'Just run it over here, Joe,' and that can get to be a hassle sometimes. I mean, I want to hear what everybody has to say and I

have confidence in everybody that they can do their jobs. But I'm the quarterback and I have to make decisions based on what is soundest at the moment. I don't want one of my teammates to think that I don't have confidence in what he can do, but still I can't go with what somebody wants if it's not the sound thing at the time. It's a tough kind of problem."

How do you handle it?

"There's no set way. Every situation is different. Take Winston Hill, for example. Winston is one of the best offensive tackles in pro football and there have been times when he's come to me during a game. 'Joe,' he'll say, and he's looking me right in the eye, 'you run that play over me and if I don't get my guy and we don't make our yards, I'll pay you $25.' I laugh a little and tell him, 'We'll get to it.' I have a great deal of confidence in Winston, but running that play might not always be the sound thing. I can usually count on Winston to get his man, but maybe the linebacker and tackle on that side are good, too, and now I need three great blocks to make that play work, not just one. Things might just be easier on the other side. Or maybe the defense is expecting us to run Winston's way. The point is, I have to try to do my job right and still be open and relate to all the guys on the team."

That seems like a tough bind.

"It is, but it gets easier the longer you do it. I've played football a long time and learned a lot about how to live and work with other people. The game has taught me a lot that I've carried over into other areas of my life. I believe in working together, doing things with other people who know how to do their part of the job, too. Talking about the other parts of my life, Jimmy Walsh takes care of the business, and he's good at it. When it's tax time, we have a specialist just to handle that. Whenever there's something I have to do, make a personal appearance or attend a meeting or something, I do that. There's a lot of us working together. I ask for help and I appreciate help and I think I learned this best in football. Out on the field, man, no matter how good you are, you can't get anything done without those ten other guys. You have your own job to do right, you have to get into your own bag out there and perform, but still it's a team thing."

Do you ever feel like you would like to engage in a sport where you didn't have to rely on other people, like boxing or long distance running?

"Overall, I just have more fun doing things with people. I like to share the excitement. When I'm down in Florida or somewhere, I can go out and shoot baskets by myself but, boy, I just love it if there's somebody else who comes along. We can play some kind of game, have some fun, and still get some good out of it."

Once in the 1972 season you were knocked down hard and your center, John Schmidt, leaned over you a long time and then helped you up and adjusted

your helmet and snapped your chin strap up.

"Yeah, I remember that. That's the way John is. He's concerned about all of his teammates."

Does it embarrass you when somebody fusses over you like that in front of people?

"No. I know what John is like. I appreciate his feelings. Sometimes I think linemen really understand football best. They're not in the limelight so they focus more on the game itself. And they know that it's all teamwork, helping each other out. It's a good feeling being part of something like that."

Joe Namath surfaced as a pop hero during the Super Season of 1968-9. He was the brash young master, the classy iconoclast, doing things the way he wanted and making it stick by doing them well. He threw the ball with daring grace and told his truth with a disarming smile and even if you didn't like what he did you had to admire the way he did it.

In an accident of timing, perhaps, the national exposure to Namath's fresh, and to some, infuriating approach concerning his appearance, his words, and his life style coincided with an upsurge in individual self-expression all across the country. He helped win the third Super Bowl just after the first great wave of the "cultural revolution" had rolled across the country from San Francisco to the East Village, leaving in its wake a legacy of long hair, free speech and free love. A typical father, enervated by his high-decibel attempts to restore his own son to the decent path of

visible collars and diligent work, was suddenly confronted with the same challenge from his Sunday television screen. Joe Namath had his hair down his neck, his social life in the newspapers and his football team in the record books. He was acting out in a green and white uniform before a high-Neilsen audience the same theory that was being advanced in less reputable circles elsewhere—you can do your own thing and still function successfully in challenging endeavors.

The sports world today is in an era of wild uniforms and footwear, of high-styled hair and flowing moustaches, and of self-confident athletes who aren't afraid to speak their minds. Namath once stood out in colorful relief against a fairly drab background, but now he is not even the most spectacular of his own teammates in terms of appearance and amusements.

Joe is not the "Compleat Swinger" and, of course, he is hardly a crash-pad hippie—not with limousines available at any of his thirteen phone extensions. Yet in may ways he is a representative member of his generation. Like many of the kids of the Sixties who are now working at being adults, Joe is still open and changing. The prefabricated answers of our society—answers like traditional grooming and good marriages and steady jobs—make no more sense to him than they do to many of his contemporaries. And again, like many of his contemporaries, he is not nearly as sure of what is coming in his future as he is that he doesn't want to live in the past.

Namath didn't start out to be a culture leader. He started out to do what he wanted, and that's still how he operates. His answers may not be the same as yours or mine, but his question is—with the old rules crumbling and the future wide open, what are we going to make of ourselves?

"There's been a lot of change in the last ten years," Joe says. "People are feeling a lot more open-minded now about what people wear, how their hair is, what their religion is, what their race is. And it's a good thing, too, because there was a lot of nonsense going on, stuff like if a guy has long hair, he can't work, or if he works at B & W Steel Mill he can't eat at a fancy restaurant, or if he is black he can't choose his seat on a bus. I guess there still is some of that, but things have certainly got better."

Why do you think that happened?

"I think that people who didn't have respect for that kind of opinion said, 'To hell with it. There's nothing wrong with what I'm doing and if people don't like it, nuts to them.' The college kids had a lot to do with this, showing you could have long hair and still be a functioning part of society. There's just more freedom now. You are able to enjoy your own taste, your own personality."

How do you mean?

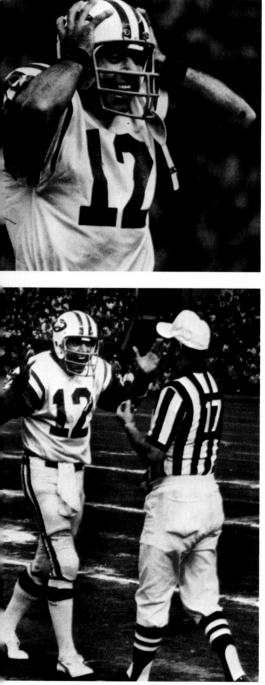

Joe has mellowed, but not so much that he lets referees err without comment

"My field is sports. Think about basketball. I love to watch those big cats do their thing out there. Ten years ago basketball had a pretty set way about it, but now those guys get up in the air and give three or four moves and slam that ball in there. They express themselves. It doesn't mean they aren't good team players. They work with the team. But when it's time to make their move, they go ahead and do it. It's beautiful to see. And things are opening up that way in other places, too. People are beginning to express themselves in the way they dress and their life style and yet they can still function, still be a part of society. I suppose we still have a long way to go, but I sure like the way it is now better than how it was in 1960."

You were one of the first to do your thing in sports with long hair and white shoes and so on. Why did you get into it?

"Something like hair style, I didn't have anybody to answer to and the shoes were a lot of fun. I had been taping my shoes on when I was in college and noticed in the films that I liked the way they looked. So I started wearing white shoes. Who else did it concern? I've always been like that. I can conform if it's time to do that. If I want to go where you have to wear a coat and tie, I wear a coat and tie. I don't want to cause any trouble because I don't want to *have* any trouble. I want to be able to move around easy, just slide in and slide out without causing a stir."

What about the demands on you like a curfew during training camp?

"That's a team thing, so it's part of my job. I don't mind curfews. I've been living with them my whole life. Now and then, of course, you have to bust out. The thing you weigh is whether it's worth the $500 fine or whatever. And if it's really time to go, buddy, you can't let a little money hold you down."

That sounds more like the Namath legend. Over the years, have you changed much?

"I've mellowed out some. Playing football, I don't get so angry at people any more. Sometimes I'll still get on a referee, but talking about the guys on the Jets, I don't get so upset. Maybe a guy gets called for holding and he's arguing with the official. I'll just say, 'Come on, man, it's over now. The official already called it.' Five years ago I might have got ticked off and yelled: 'Shut the hell up! What are you holding for in the first place?' But what good does that do? If the guy knows he made a mistake, that's all that's necessary, and if the ref blew one we just have to keep working anyway."

What about off the field?

"It's the same. I don't get as excited any more. Maybe somebody writes something stupid in the newspapers. I've been through a lot of that and I've found it just doesn't do any good to get upset. People are still going to write garbage and other people are still going to believe it."

You feel that the newspapers have created an image of you that isn't true, that you would like to change?

"No, that's not it. Most of the things that you have read about me, I've done things like that at one time or another. It's just that usually the stories you hear and the things I've done don't go together at the same times in the same places with the same people. And even if the various incidents people have heard about me are usually wrong, if I think about the image I have in public, I really wouldn't change anything."

Do you ever deliberately play at being Joe Namath, the guy people have read about?

"Sometimes I've done that. Maybe I'll meet some people in a bar and they'll start kidding around with me and I'll get into it and come on strong and have a good time. If people like you, if they want to laugh at you because you make them happy, well good. Make them laugh. Or sometimes I come on as Joe Namath because it can help me get a good seat at a club or something. You do that. I took my father to see Elvis Presley in Las Vegas once. My father is a big fan of Elvis. We got a good table and then afterward I asked him if he wanted to meet Elvis. He did, naturally, and so I just told the people to ask if Joe Namath could come backstage and my dad got to meet Elvis and they sat and talked for a long time. I think Elvis is great, a nice dude, and my father loved it and that made me happy."

That seems like a positive use of your image.

"Yeah. If being Joe Namath can bring somebody pleasure for some part of time, well, then, I'm happy to do it."

2 pictures of elegance

Joe Namath has an elegant throwing motion. That was the word that seemed right to me—elegant—and when I looked it up in the American Heritage Dictionary the first definition listed was "refinement and grace in motion." Exactly.

Joe's style is highly refined. There are no excesses, and no disconnections. He gets maximum results with minimum effort because all the parts of his body—legs, hips, shoulders, left arm, right arm—work smoothly and solidly together. Standing next to him as he throws, there is a feeling of power that is perfectly harnessed and directed.

His is not the classic style. Perhaps Bart Starr had that, the solid plant on the right foot, the deliberate step toward the target and the precise overhand delivery. But there is definitely a grace to Namath's motion, a smooth style that seems almost to belong to a dancer. Because he moves so quickly on the field, some of the beauty goes by too swiftly to be seen in person, but in still photographs the elegance emerges: the swooping stop to his dropback with weight curved forward and ready, the swirling turn of the delivery itself, the floating fade-away that is his unique follow-through.

It is probably presumptuous to call him an artist, but he is surely a fine craftsman and he has created a motion that is not only pleasing to watch but almost perfectly suited to the task he is faced with.

It was considerations like these which led us to the decision to go to Johnny Zimmerman, one of America's most respected photographers, to capture Namath's motion with the technical artistry of stroboscopic photography. As a cameraman Zimmerman is equally at home with the instantaneous excitement of outdoor action or the more deliberate wizardry of studio sessions, and a week of his round-the-clock work using seventy thousand dollars worth of equipment produced the following unique portfolio.

His photographs are a fitting tribute to Namath's style. Like the motion they portray, they are both attractive and functional. The multiple exposures produce a pleasing pattern of their own; and the superimposed images afford an otherwise unattainable view of the simplicity and rhythm of Namath's form.

Facing page: *Joe starts his motion with the green stripes on the side of his pants facing at his target and his left shoulder cocked under his chin. Then he whips his hips around and turns the shoulders and the ball comes out over the top with a clean and powerful arm action. The images here cover a span of little more than four tenths of a second.*
Overleaf: *In a side view, Joe's simple arm action becomes obvious. The ball goes straight up and out with no up-and-down hitch and no backward motion behind the head, thus allowing the quickest possible release.*

"I take it for granted
that I look good throw-
ing, that I have good
form. That's how
I know my motion is
easy and natural. Any
time I start to look
awkward throwing,
I know I'm doing
something wrong."

Facing page: *In an unusual over-
head view, it is possible to see the
circular nature of Namath's release.
He has the ball cocked at the top
of the picture, with his left shoulder
facing the target, and he unwinds in
a counterclockwise direction with
his left elbow leading around.
He does not follow through in the
direction of the throw, but instead
he keeps turning considerably
beyond the line the ball takes
toward the target.*

3 a passer's style

The circle and the spiral are the basic forms of motion in nature. From the swarming electrons in atomic structure to the streaming galaxies of outer space, centrifugal motion is an ever-repeating pattern.

It would not be surprising to find that centrifugal motion would also be a natural action for the human body any time both precision and power were needed and, indeed, baseball hitters, golfers, even a shot putter all use variations on a compact and efficient rotation of the body.

It is in this context that Joe Namath's throwing motion makes the most sense. Although he looks unusual for a quarterback, since quarterbacks typically throw with a more straight-line forward motion, he fits right in with athletes in other sports. Like batters and golfers and shot putters, he uses a motion that is keyed to a powerful turn of the hips and shoulders with the arms in close to the body and all the action simple and compact.

The efficiency of his style stands out strikingly when it is compared to that of other accurate passers. John Unitas skips forward and flips the ball out with an exaggerated overhand throwing motion—very straight line. Sonny Jurgensen round-houses the ball with a huge arc in his arm. Sammy Baugh used to face square downfield and sidearm the ball. Norm Van Brocklin used to bring it back near his ear and then push it out as much as fling it.

All these people are or have been great passers, but it does not seem logical to try to teach anybody else to throw like they do. Each of their motions is a little awkward and their passing success seems to be something of a triumph of athletic ability over physical principles.

Namath's style, on the other hand, is physically logical. All parts of his body are working together in a simple action that puts power on the ball all out of proportion to the amount of energy he seems to put into it.

Apparently there has never been an attempt to discuss a passing motion in great detail before, but maybe that's because no style ever really made this much sense. There have been many books on the golfing swing and many on hitting a baseball— Ted Williams' is probably the best—and perhaps it is because Namath's throw has so much in common with these ideas that they lend themselves to this sort of analysis.

In any event, between the pictures and Namath's words, we hope the main ideas can be understood. The following section is structured so the armchair quarterback can pick up the main thoughts from the pictures and captions. But for the field quarterback, we did our best to include all the details that would make the motion a realistic possibility.

my way

I throw the ball differently from most quarterbacks. I'm talking about the physical throwing motion, the way I use my body and arm. It's different from what I see other people doing and I think it has a lot of advantages. Instead of moving my weight forward and whipping the ball with my arm, like a lot of quarterbacks, I turn my weight in a circle and throw with a very short arm motion.

I never really noticed the difference until I got into pro ball. Back in high school and college I wasn't thinking too much about it. Hell, I was just setting and throwing and trying to win games. But when I got to the pros I began to hear a lot of talk about how I had a quick release and how I had a short motion. I started looking at other cats throwing the ball in the films and I began to see that there really is a difference. I don't look the same throwing as other guys. They use their feet differently, they have a lot more motion in their arm sometimes, they don't use their bodies the same.

And after looking at those films, I had to agree with what I was hearing. It does seem like what I'm doing is usually a little quicker, like people say. Maybe it's only two or three tenths of a second but that's a lot when those guys are coming at you in the pocket. When we took pictures for this book at the rate of ten a second, we saw that from the time I begin to step to the time the ball is actually leaving my hand, the whole throwing motion takes only half a second. **What other advantages are there besides quickness?**

When I began to think about

the way I was throwing the ball I saw that being quick isn't the only advantage to it. The way I throw has a lot of advantages. It keeps me from stepping up into the rush. It lets me throw at the last instant. It helps me throw certain kinds of passes even if I'm off balance and I haven't quite got my feet together.

What I'm saying is I think a lot of guys could get some help by paying attention to what I'm doing even if they don't copy me exactly. I know football people often say it's best just to leave a quarterback alone, that the natural motion is the best motion. But I don't know. It seems to me that if the natural way a guy throws—the way he just happened to start when he first picked up a ball—is a long way away from the quickest and simplest way, then he can help himself by working on his motion. Any quarterback has to have some natural talent, of course, and he has to want to spend a lot of his life practicing. But somewhere in there getting a good motion is awfully important.

What I do is maybe a little weird, compared to how most guys do it, and the details are hard to pick up without some explanation. But between the photographs and what I've got to say here, I think we can get it all clear, and all I can say is I think it's worth the effort.

There are a lot of pictures of me looking over my left shoulder because I have to coil my body up in order to turn as I throw. I have to practice hard on all stages of the throw every year.

The way I throw is simple and quick but getting myself ready to do it that way isn't simple or quick at all. There's a lot of stuff to work on, a lot of little details about footwork, using my weight, my arm motion and especially the way I turn my body when I release the ball. There are so many things to get together you can't get it all solved in a few weeks, or even a few months. Every year I have to start over, working on first one part of it and then another, building myself up in stages. And the goal is to cut out all waste motion, to get everything functioning right now, right now, right now. What you want is an instant throw.

If you go back to step one and get the basics together, then you can go ahead and free lance. You practice each stage separately and then you put them together and when the games come and it's the time to roll you can just fly right into it. No thinking or getting ready. You already know what you are doing. It's a matter of mentally going through it and going through it, and mechanically practicing and practicing, and then when everything comes naturally you just turn yourself loose.

grip

I take the ball with my fingers across the laces. Every quarter-back I ever saw does the same, although I guess some guys used to throw with their thumb on the laces and other ways. Actually it's only the little finger that really hooks the laces hard. The little finger isn't all that strong and if you can hook it on the laces well, it gives you strength in that part of the grip. Your index finger and thumb are stronger and more coordinated and they don't need the help as much as that little finger.

I spread my fingers out maximum, or close to maximum. You want those fingers wide to grab as much of the ball as you can, but be careful you don't overstretch.

Sometimes I've heard guys say you should emphasize grabbing the ball with your fingertips and not let your palm touch the ball. Other guys say palm the ball, get right up next to it. But I don't think you should pay that much attention to whether you are palming the ball or not. What you should pay attention to is whether you have control of the ball. Maybe the heel of your hand doesn't quite touch the ball most of the time—and I'm talking about it's a sixteenth of an inch off, or something like that—but it might touch in some parts of your motion or on some throws. It's nothing to worry about, though, it's nothing to emphasize. Emphasize control. How does the ball feel in your hand as you throw?

How can you adjust your grip?

You might notice that if you are using too much fingertip or choking down too close to the tip end of the ball, where it's not so fat, you have trouble getting your body into the throw and really getting authority into the ball. When I have to throw the ball hard, I don't like to grip it near the end. I feel I have more control of it by gripping it nearer the center.

On the other hand, if you have the ball on your palm too much, or hold the ball too far toward the middle where it's fat, you don't have enough touch in your fingers. The ball is just laying in in your hand too much. Then you will notice that you shove the ball as you throw it, push it a little bit like a shot-putter, or maybe you sort of sling it side-arm. The ball doesn't feel crisp as it leaves your fingers. If that is happening, maybe you should emphasize your fingertips more, see if you can't feel more control of the ball as it leaves your hand.

Again, control is the test. Don't go looking at the space between your palm and the ball to see how big it is. Feel it. Get solid control. When you start turning your whole body behind the throw, there will be a lot of strain on your grip. It can't be too delicate or too mushy. Keep experimenting and adjusting. As you change your throwing motion or as your arm gets stronger, you may want to adjust your grip to transmit more power to the ball. Do it. Work out a way for yourself where you can get maximum control.

My fingers are spread and I try to get a solid feeling of control over the ball so it leaves my hand in a firm, powerful manner.

stance

The way to stand up there behind the center is just whatever way you feel comfortable. I know personally I don't look much like one of these textbook stances. Hell, I'm round-shouldered and I'm sort of bent over up there, but I can get done what I have to and it feels comfortable to me.

A couple of things seem important to me. First I want to have my legs spread some and the feet about even. I have to turn both ways, depending on what kind of play it is, so I need to have my feet even. I may stagger my feet sometimes—if there's a guard pulling in my direction to block for instance, I need that foot out of the way. But I don't do it often because the defense might pick it up. I like my legs spread pretty wide. In college I used to have them really wide, outside of the center's feet, but then I decided I could get up a little higher and see a little better if I brought them in a little. I'm still spread out more than most guys.

Another thing is I want to have my legs bent slightly at the knees. I want some flexion in there because then I feel as if I'm already coiled up and ready to explode. This should put your weight on the balls of your feet, even though your heels may not be off the ground. You don't move out straight-legged. You need something to push from and you can't push out if your legs are already straight. But if you get some leg flex in your stance, and your weight on the balls of your feet, then you're already there, and you don't waste any motion pushing out. You are ready to explode right from where you are.

I want my stance comfortable, with legs bent, feet spread, and weight up on my toes. My hands dig in deep under center to insure a solid exchange of the ball.

dropback

My dropback into the pocket got messed up by my first knee operation. I could still run back all right but I had to change the way I stopped and set up. There have been a lot of problems caused by that knee, but this is one place where I think it helped me. The way I set up now is unusual but I really think it's the right way to do things.

I've heard people say I get back into the pocket faster than anybody else. Maybe so, maybe not, but the way I set up is certainly no accident. When I take that ball from center, boy, I turn and SPRINT back. I mean I'm just all-out racing. I don't get any gold medals for getting back into the pocket fast, but I do get myself maybe two or three tenths of a second to get set and be sure of what I'm going to do with the ball. That time is important. You want to be quick when you're back there throwing, but you don't want to be rushing yourself.

What are the key factors in the dropback?

I do two or three things differently on the dropback than a lot of quarterbacks. First is that I turn almost all the way around with my back to the defense. Some people keep their head and upper body around and facing the defense more and they sort of crab back into the pocket sideways. I know what their thinking is. They want to see as much of the defense as they can so they can read the pass coverage. But twisting around like that has to slow them down. You can't face one way and sprint the other way. And in most cases I know I can read all the defense I need while turning and going in an all-out sprint. I can look back over my shoulder and see half the field easily—a cornerman, both safeties, and two linebackers. On the passes where I need to see more—and there aren't many—I use a backpedal. But on most passes, it seems to me, speed back into the pocket is more important than seeing the whole field.

Another thing I do that isn't all that common is that I carry the ball one-handed after the first couple of steps. It doesn't bother me to do that because with my grip, I know I have control of the ball. And I like to do it. I think it helps because—like I say—I am going back into that pocket full steam. You can't run all out with your two hands holding a ball in front of your chest. You have to pump your arms to get your speed going and so that's what I do. I'm not sure I'd recommend it for a kid starting out. His hand may not be large enough to have a secure grip.

The third thing I do, the thing that is probably most unusual, is that when I get back my seven yards I stop myself and come to a set on my left leg. This is the thing that was forced on me by my operation. The natural thing for any man to do when he is running back and turning this way is to stop by sticking out his right foot. Most quarterbacks do this. Even though I had no choice I believe stopping on my left leg is one of the keys to my whole style. Let's go through the dropback step by step and then I'll tell you why I think so when we get to the set up.

How do you start away from center?

The first couple of steps are vital to a quick drop. I want to get my weight moving backward as fast as possible. It may sound a little odd, but the way I get myself going is that I "sit down" into the turn away from center.

To make any move like this quickly you have to keep your weight low, and to do that you have to keep your rear end low. The way I get going is to sit back a little and whip my right side around and back, just pull my right elbow and my right hip backwards as fast as I can. Between sitting and yanking my right side backwards I've got a good quick, low start.

At the same time I'm sitting down, I'm driving off my right foot. I usually take a little false step forward with my right foot and then drive off it. Most quarterbacks do this. I've tried to stop it sometimes, because it seems like waste motion, but every time in a game it comes back, so it must be natural.

I drop back to pass in a full-speed race and then set up to throw in an unusual manner: I stop with most of my weight on my left leg, my front leg, and that means I'm ready to throw without unnecessary steps.

1

2

3

4

5

6

Pushing off like that, the thigh muscles and the calf muscles and the toes really fire out full blast. Those first steps are an all-out effort, like an explosion. On the first step I really shove off with the left leg all the way down to the toes. I land on the toes of my right foot and really shove off again. I already have my weight working with me because of the way I have "sat down" into the start and yanked my side around, and I keep it that way by staying low and leaning forward in the direction I'm running. The first step covers about a yard and the second one a little more, and they make the difference in how fast my drop is going to be.

How many steps are there in the drop?

My normal seven-yard drop consists of seven steps altogether. I'm sure this might change depending on the quarterback but for anybody close to my height— 6-1—who is running back there all out, I think it would work out about the same.

After I've pushed off hard with my left leg and then my right one, on the next two steps I land more flatfooted and just keep my momentum up rather than forcing for even greater speed. Where I was staying low and leaning forward a lot, now I raise up a little and my weight comes back more over my center of gravity.

To start away from center, I sit down a little to get my weight moving, use a quick push-off step with my right foot and yank my right side back and around.

How do you stop and set up?

Here's where we get to the business of stopping on my left leg. At the end of the fourth stride, I get that left leg out in front of me almost stiff straight, jam my heel into the turf and break most of my momentum right there. My right leg comes through on a short step and then I reach out with my left leg again and really bring myself to a stop. Again, to help me stop, I "sit down"—lower my rear end—and lean way back toward the line of scrimmage.

By the time my right leg trails out behind me on the seventh "step," all the work is done. The toe of that foot tips down, but there isn't much weight on it. My weight is all forward and I'm sitting down on my left leg.

How did the knee problem affect the dropback?

Those last four steps are kind of an uneven gallop. They go LEFT-right-LEFT-right. BOOM-tip BOOM-tip. The left leg is taking all the strain. The reason for this, of course, goes back to the way I tore up my right knee during my senior year in college. By the time I got an operation, that knee was already in bad shape and it has never been able to carry its share of the weight since. That's why I got into stopping on my left leg when I came to the pros. It was the only way I could do things. But over the years I've come to realize there was one blessing in that torn up right knee. Stopping on the left leg is the best way to do things and my only problem now is keeping that left leg healthy enough.

Why is it good to stop on the left leg?

When I stop on my left leg I am stopping on my forward leg, the one that is most in the direction that I am going to throw.

The trouble with guys who stop on the right leg, the back leg, is that then they've got their weight back. Before they can throw, they have to shift their weight up forward. That wastes time. Stopping on your back foot is almost like stepping back into a hole. Before you can throw, first you have to climb out.

My right leg trails out and catches the last remaining part of my momentum and then I straighten up some off my left leg. I'll talk about this some more in the section on footwork. But the important thing for now is that I don't want to stop on my right leg. When I do that I tend to have my weight too far back and my legs get too spread out, and that's not a comfortable position to throw from.

People sometimes think I take a specially deep drop, but I think that's because of the way I stop like this with my weight already forward and ready to go. When I stop at seven yards, I'm solid right there. I don't move back up into the pocket to get my weight moving forward, so maybe it looks like I'm deeper than some other people. Occasionally I'll drop deeper than seven yards, but only if I absolutely know that I'm going to throw deep.

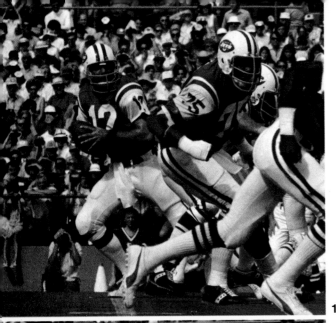

I come out with my back to the
defense, leaning forward and driving.

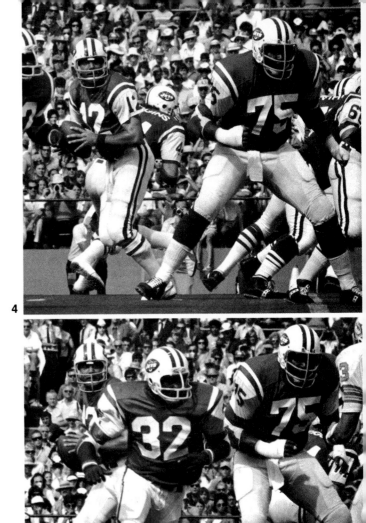

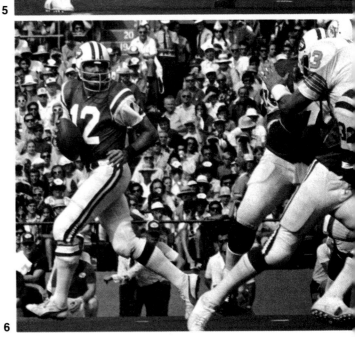

In the middle steps, I straighten up,
center my weight and maintain my speed.

76

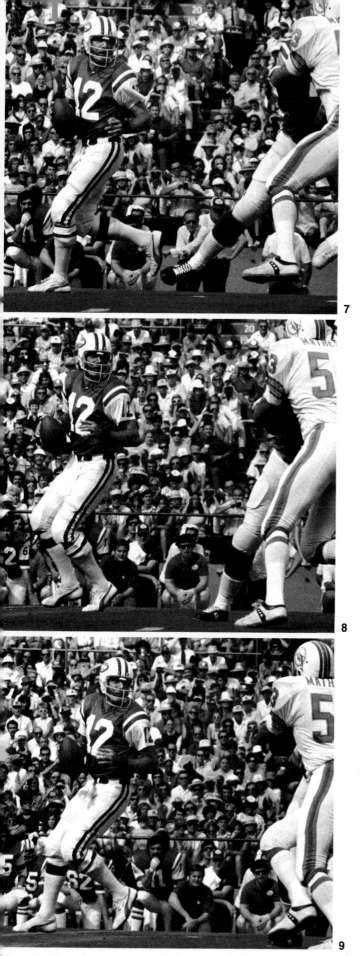

7

8

9

The ball is in one hand as I begin to brake
with my left leg on the fourth step.

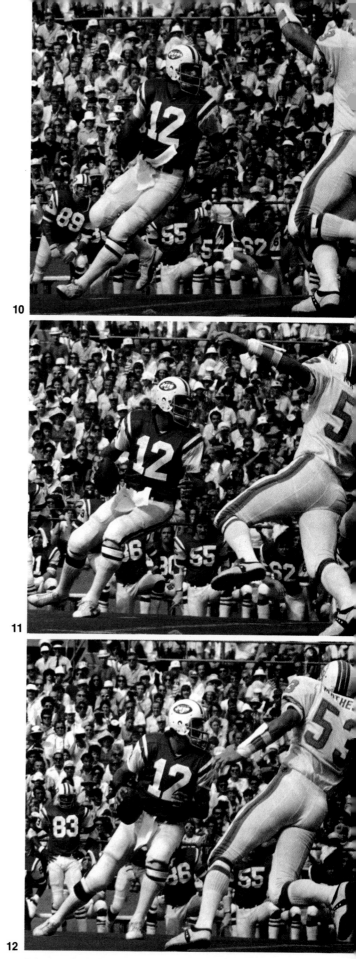

10

11

12

I lean back toward the line and stop
over my left leg with my weight forward.

I don't have to go blasting back seven yards on all types of passes, of course. On some passes, such as quick outs and short slants to my wide receivers, or quick passes to my backs, I only need to take a few steps and then unload right then.

The basic ideas are still the same. On a three-step dropback, I turn and go hard but at the end of the second step my left heel is jamming into the ground already and I'm sitting down back toward the line of scrimmage. My right leg comes through for the third step and this time it really takes some weight. A short pass happens so fast there is no time to get stopped over the left leg. I just keep moving and my left foot has to take a real step as I throw, either out to the right or all the way around to the left. The most important things are for me to keep my hips low and, on a throw to the right, to be sure to get my left shoulder cocked all the way to the right.

On short passes I start back hard but then I stop so quickly that I really have to use the right leg.

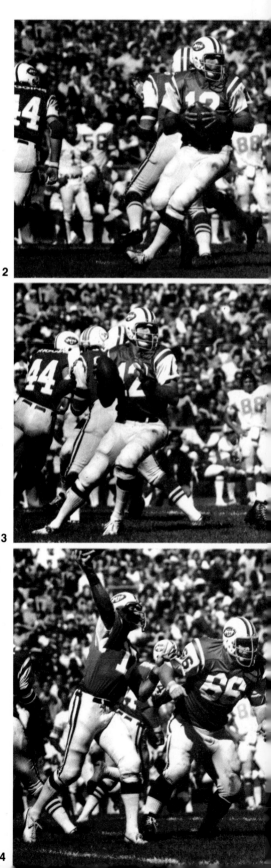

2

3

backpedal

Sometimes I just can't get the job done if I turn my back and race seven yards for my set-up. Maybe I have to see way out to my left and watch the linebacker on that side especially. Maybe I'm thinking he might blitz and I want to watch him. Or maybe I'm going to throw right into his area and I have to know exactly where he is going.

If that's what's happening, instead of turning and running back into the pocket, I just scoot backward to my set-up spot. This is backpedaling—running backwards while facing the line of scrimmage.

I don't recommend this move for young quarterbacks. Usually it's not necessary because they don't have to read the defenses the way the pros must. And for sure it's very awkward. It's much more important to polish up a quick and efficient dropback than it is to fool around with a backpedal. But at the professional level I feel that the backpedal is necessary now and then and I've worked on it a lot to make it as smooth as possible.

How is the backpedal done?

There's not much technique to the getting back. I just lean out backward, so my weight is pulling me, and I scoot backward as fast as I can make my feet move. It isn't the way your legs were made to do things, but if defensive backs can learn it, so can quarterbacks. It's slower than an all-out sprint but it can happen pretty quickly with practice.

Setting up is the really tough part of the backpedal. The first thing is that I have to make sure I get my weight leaning on my left leg as I stop and then

On the backpedal, I lean out backward and scoot, then lean forward again and stop with my weight forward, being careful to cock my left shoulder to the right if I must throw to my right.

straighten up. I lean backward as I'm moving backward, but on the last couple of steps I really tip my weight over forward again and I stop with my weight out over my left leg just like I do on the normal dropback.

Weight distribution is the key. If I don't lean backward at first, I won't get any speed, and if I don't lean forward as I stop, I won't get anything on the throw—I'll be throwing while still falling backward.

The other awkward thing about the backpedal is that I go back with my shoulders square downfield. That wouldn't be so bad if I were a quarterback who threw the ball with a straight overarm flip, but it's really tough on my style since I throw by turning my body. Before I can throw off the backpedal, I have to cock my left shoulder around to the right and then whip it back around to the left.

Mainly, the backpedal is a drag. I keep trying to get away from it, but there's just some times in the pro game where I have to use it. My advice is don't mess with it until you have to.

the throw

1 Before the throwing motion starts, the body is sitting down slightly with the left hip and shoulder turned around to the right. The ball is held away from the body and about chest high.

2 The left leg begins to step and the step is to the left of the target.

3 Both arms raise up together and the hips begin to turn, but the shoulders remain coiled.

**nearly beside
even before the
he ground.
not reaching
front of the
—not overstrid-
ettling in close to
ght to be trans-
left foot easily.**

4 The hips begin to whip around although the shoulders are still closed. The ball is at full height and although it has been raised straight up, it is left behind a little by the body action.

5 The left elbow has pulled around hard and the shoulders have begun a powerful turn, but the ball is still left behind in about the same position. This allows the ball to be cocked without it ever being moved backward.

4 The ball is coming smoothly straight up and the left arm and shoulder have begun to pull around as the left foot tips the ground.

5 The body weight moves quickly from right to left, instead of from back to front, and the left arm continues to pull across. The ball is raised to the cocked position.

6 The hip whip and shoulder turn are at full power as the ball is slammed forward. The left side is out of the way and the right side is rolling forward.

7 The wrist snaps forward with the throw. It does not rotate. The left hip is pulling backward so hard, as the right side goes forward, that the left leg actually straightens up some, pulling the weight back off the left toe.

8 The turn rolls on around into the follow through, with the left elbow still leading and the right arm finished across the body.

1 Although the weight is balanced on the right foot, the center of gravity is forward. The weight is never shifted back to the right side. The power of the throw comes from turning, not moving forward. The ball is carried chest high.

2 The left arm and shoulder close to the right slightly more as the left leg begins the step. The ball begins to move up at the same time.

3 The ball the hea left foot hits The left leg i far forward i body weight ing—but is s allow the we ferred to the

6 The hips and shoulders are turning strongly and suddenly the arm has snapped up and out, driving the ball forward.

7 The backward turn of the left hip continues and the left toe comes up off the ground. The weight is pivoting on the left heel.

8 The left foot has turned outward considerably and the body has gone on around in a turn that is more than 180 degrees. Even in the follow through, the center of gravity is still behind the left foot as the weight turns on around and back away from the line of scrimmage.

turning the body

I throw the ball by wheeling my body around in a circle, by opening up my hips and shoulders as I throw and then following on around to my left.

What I do is step out to my left a little on most passes instead of straight ahead. I lean a little to the left, getting my momentum going right-to-left, then wheel my body around hard. It's a circular motion instead of a straight ahead motion.

When I say I turn my body, I mean just that. I turn all the way around—180 degrees—on most passes and further than that on some of those deep ones out to the left. When I start to throw my left shoulder is cocked in front of my chin. My body is completely "closed," coiled and ready to open up, to unwind around in a circle.

As I start to throw I step out to my left a little, like a batter who steps in the bucket. My hips start to open up hard to my left and so do my left arm and shoulders. My right arm comes up and slams the ball forward when my body turn is at maximum power.

How does the body turn?

My whole body seems to whip around at once, but maybe my hips really start just a little in front. The whip from the hips is where the power all starts. With those hips turning, the center of gravity of the body is moving at the core of the turn. If the shoulders turn without the hips, the body is sort of fighting itself, and the motion is weak. But if the hips are whipping under the shoulders and the

whole body is coming on around, all the power available is being put to use.

They've got a phrase in golf, "Have a quick belly button." Jerk those hips around, get enough motion to where the belly button winds farther around even than the direction the ball took. Get the whole power of your body behind the ball.

I finish my throw with my right side facing the target and now I'm looking out over my right shoulder to see what happens. It's a complete turn. My belt buckle is facing one way when I start and the other way when I'm done. My receiver can read the number on my left shoulder as I start and the number on my right shoulder as I finish.

Do other passers turn their body?

Most throwers turn their bodies to some extent. Some don't, of course. It's really hard to throw the ball at all without turning to some extent.

But I am definitely an extreme case. Almost all my power comes from the turn itself. I don't push forward with my back foot like most throwers and my weight really doesn't move forward much at all on most throws. When I'm done throwing, especially on throws to my left, I fall away to my left or even to my left and backward away from the line.

The reason my weight doesn't go forward is that my left side pulls around and backward just as hard as my right side turns around forward.

My left elbow and shoulder pull backward and so does my left hip. The faster that left side pulls back, the faster my right

side turns forward and the harder I can throw the ball. But as for my own body moving anywhere, the result is a near stalemate. I fall away to the left sometimes because I lean that way. As for forward momentum, I really don't have much at all.

What are the problems with throwing this way?

The thing I have to watch out for throwing like this is to keep my turn together. Everything has to happen in one piece, all together. If I get my left side turning too soon and get out in front of my arm, I wind up too "open." When I throw across my body that way, I use too much arm because the momentum from the turn has already been mostly used up. That will sometimes happen when I'm throwing out to my left. It's all arm because the body did its work too soon.

Throwing out to my right, two different things can go wrong. One thing is I can start to throw without ever really getting coiled up, without getting my left side all the way around and facing out to the right toward the target. This is a big danger when I backpedal into the pocket, running backward while facing square downfield. If I do backpedal and want to throw to my right, I have to remember to turn my left side all the way around to the right, to close up, before I

My weight does not move forward much as I throw; it turns in a circle with my left arm and hip pulling back as fast as my right arm and hip come forward. I do have to be careful (above) not to turn my body too soon and leave my arm behind.

start to throw. If I don't get closed before I start to throw, I can't get any power from turning my body and opening up toward my receiver. I deliberately throw this pass a few times in pre-game warmups and occasionally in games, just to show the other people I can do it off the back-pedal when I have to.

The other thing that can happen when I'm throwing to my right is that I get hung up a little and can't turn my body all the way around. Throwing to the right while turning to the left can sometimes be a problem. It's hard to get the left side all the way around and out of the way. On throws to the right I usually don't turn as much as I do throwing over the center or out to the left.

Another thing I have to be careful of throwing this way is that I don't let my turn pull the ball too far off to the left. I'm wheeling left hard and that is the tendency, to pull the ball left. If I stepped straight ahead and threw right over the top I imagine my trouble would be up-and-down, having the ball go too high or too low. But throwing with this turning motion, the problem is more side-to-side, keeping the ball from flying away there too far to the left.

Bubba Smith was coming (right) but I have already turned my left hip and shoulder hard, come through with my right side and released this bomb down the right sideline with almost no forward motion.

arm action

I don't use much throwing motion. Some people say I have a short motion, but I'm not sure this describes it too well. The thing is, I try to have no excess movement in there at all, no flips or hitches or windups or anything like that. I just bring the ball up to my ear and go.

I got into that when I was small. My older brothers taught me how to throw and they always emphasized that I should just bring the ball up and throw right from my ear. Bring it up and throw, bring it up and throw. No windup. Don't drop the ball down behind your head. Right from the ear.

I listened to them and I tried to do that and it just became natural. Get the ball up and just slam it out there. Of course, I don't think this would make as much sense if it weren't for the way I twist my body when I throw. I get so much power from my body that I don't need to get into a lot of action with my arm.

Other guys who don't use their weight the same way might have to wind up more with their arm, use more of a whip or a wrist flip or something. But I don't need to do that. I get all the power I need on the ball just with a simple nailing motion in my arm because I have so much body in there behind the throw. I don't really know why I got into the body twist, but it was probably just because I was trying to use such a simple, quick arm action, like my brothers were telling me, that I had to do something to get some power into the throw.

Where is the ball carried before the throw?

I try to carry the ball up pretty high. I want to have it up around my chest as I'm getting set to throw. I want to have it up fairly close to where I'm going to go with the ball to release it. If it's hanging down too low as I start to throw, my body turn gets going before I can get the ball up and ready to go. Then my arm gets behind my body because it has to bring the ball so far up. And I wind up more flinging the ball than really nailing it. I don't get on top of the throw, and the throw is weaker because the timing is off. So I always try to carry the ball high as I set up, where I can just pick it up a little beside my ear and go right now.

Why is a hitch bad?

But even more important than keeping the ball high, I believe, is making sure that I don't hitch as I start to throw. What I mean by that is I don't want to have the ball up fairly high and then drop it down a little just before I raise it up to throw. A lot of guys do that, the way a lot of hitters kind of bounce their bats up and down just before the swing. These passers usually carry that ball high, up by their heads, but their throwing motion then goes down-up-out. I even do it now and then. It's sort of natural, like a mini-windup, like you might pick up a rock and flip and throw. But it's really bad, boy. At least I think it is. It's a waste of time, in the first place, and like I say even one-tenth of a second matters a lot. In the second place, the way I throw coordinating arm action with body turn, a hitch is excess motion that gets in the way. If I were throwing with more emphasis on my arm for power, I suppose I could let my arm flop and hitch more because the arm would be doing the work alone. But the way I throw, my arm is working with my body. When my body gets around there, my arm has to be ready to go. I don't want it jumping up and down in a hitch just when I need it. Everything has to be all together, all in one piece.

What is the correct motion?

Instead of my arm going down-up-out — three motions — I really want it to go up-and-out — all one motion. As I'm raising the ball my shoulders are already turning and by the time the ball gets up beside my head it's time to go right then. Up-and-out, all at once.

Throwing a rock or a baseball, your arm can be a lot looser, have more whip in it. But a football is bulky and awkward. It's hard to move it around a lot and still keep control of it and keep your timing together.

I throw by using a simple, powerful nailing motion of my arm without letting my wrist turn or twist as the ball comes up and starts forward.

How does twisting the wrist hurt a spiral?

Besides, throwing a football you've got a problem you don't have with a rock or a baseball. You've got to make that thing spiral. The more motion you have in your arm and wrist while you're getting ready to throw, the more difficult it gets to have a spiral. If your arm and wrist are flipping and twisting in your windup, chances are the ball will go out the same way—with a flopping wobble on it. When some guys throw, there's a time in their motion when they have their wrist turned outward quite a lot, so the ball is up near their head with the back of their hand turned in toward their head. It's all a part of a whip they are putting on the ball. Now I know that if you've thrown this way a long time, you can get to where you can do that and still get a spiral most of the time. But I don't think it's a good idea. It's just one more motion to keep together, one more thing that can go wrong if you are rushed. I know if I let my wrist turn out a little like that, it makes it harder to throw a spiral. I have to close the wrist up again as I'm throwing and that makes the ball wobble.

I don't ever want my wrist to turn out and then twist back in. I want to keep my wrist closed all the time. I try to keep the ball pointed in the direction I'm going to throw all through the motion. I know if you look at the pictures (pages 82-85) it doesn't really look that way. The ball is actually pointing out to the side

when it's up by my head instead of pointing in the direction it will go. But that's not because my wrist is turned. It's because my shoulders are turned. As my shoulders come around in the throw, the ball comes around to point at the target naturally without me moving my wrist or forearm. That's the key: no excess motion. To me as I'm throwing the ball, it feels in my hand as though the ball is always pointed right down the throwing line. My wrist has no outward turn just before I start forward and there is no strain on my grip. Again, I'm just nailing the ball, throwing with the simplest arm action I can so it can be quick and fit right in with my body.

Why shouldn't the arm be cocked backward?

There's another part to this that also keeps the strain off my grip and keeps my motion simple and together. When I take that ball to throw, I don't drop it down behind my head or shoulder. I don't take the ball back and then snap it forward. It goes up-and-out. The ball never moves down or backward.

If you drop the ball back and then flip it out, there's a strain put on your grip. You pull the ball quickly in one direction—backward—then suddenly reverse the motion and whip it out forward. That's hard. It's physically a difficult thing to do.

This is another place where the photographs can lie a little bit if you don't look at them carefully. If you look at the shots of my arm just before I start my forward motion, you will see that the ball is not really beside my ear. It's behind my head some. But what I'm saying is still true. I don't cock my arm backward. The ball never is moving backward.

Look closely at the photos (page 82-85). You'll notice that even though the ball is behind my head at one point in time, still it is very high. I never drop it down behind me. My arm stays at about a right angle—about 90 degrees—and never folds up much more than that.

The next thing to see is that the ball doesn't get behind me because I pull it back. It gets behind me because my body turns away from it. To me it seems like I'm raising that ball straight up to my ear. But because the left side of my body has already started to turn to the left, turn counterclockwise, the ball gets left behind a little bit. What happens is I get the ball cocked behind me for free. I don't have to do anything to get the ball cocked. I never move it backward. My arm action is super simple, just up-and-out, and I get this little whipping action as a natural bonus. My body is turning as I raise the ball and by the time the ball is up and ready to go, it is left behind a little. Then I slam it forward as my body keeps on going around. By using a body turn I get the best of both worlds—a simple arm motion and a little arm whip at the same time with no strain on my grip.

1

2

3

4

My arm starts up at the same time that I step out to the left and the ball goes smoothly up and out with no unnecessary hitches — in less than four-tenths of a second.

Why should the ball be kept in close to the head?

Since I'm talking about throwing in a circle, some people might think the ball is sort of flung out wide around in a circle, that you take it out away from your head and bring it around in an arc while your body turns around.

But that's not the way I do it at all. My arm action is actually pretty straight. It's just that nailing motion. The thing is, I bring the ball right up next to my head to start with and then snap it outward on a straight line. I stay inside and then snap out like a right-handed batter slashing the ball to right center.

How does the left arm help the throw?

My left arm is almost as important as my right one. That might sound weird, but look at the pictures. The way I use my left arm is important all through my whole throwing motion. I throw by turning my body, opening up as I throw, and my left side has to pull around and out of the way in order for my right side to come through.

But if you look at the pictures, you can see how my left arm works for me. As I raise the ball up with my right hand, I also raise my left arm up almost as high as my face. My elbow is a little lower than my hand and the arm is bent up pretty well. As I start to come around to throw, my left arm pulls around, down and back. It stays together in that solid position, bent at the elbow, and it almost seems like it is pulling my shoulders around. The left arm, shoulders and my whole upper body stay solid, in one piece, as I turn.

You can also see how the left arm helps to get the right arm up higher for the release. As my hips start turning, the left arm pulls around and down. That left elbow seems to dive down and around behind my hip. As it does that, it pulls my left shoulder down, too, and so my right shoulder and arm get pulled up. My shoulders are tipped unevenly with the left one pulled down much lower than the right. That's how I can get a high release even though I don't throw overhand. My right arm extends from my shoulder almost sideways, but because my shoulders are tipped over, the right arm is actually sticking up high in the air.

This is my strongest throwing position. This is the way I go when I really have to get that ball out there, throwing deep outs or deep slants, anything where the ball has to get there right now. When I know I've got that kind of pass coming up I tell myself to get good and high, get on top of the ball, and the power all comes out. I couldn't really tell you why, analyze the geometry of it or anything. But I know it's true and if you try it you'll feel how it works.

When that ball comes off my fingers, I want it to feel solid and powerful. I take the ball up there and slam it out, pound it out. It's almost as though I had a stake in my hand, a pole a couple of inches in diameter and maybe a foot long.

Imagine you have a stake in your hand like that and you're holding it like a spear and you want to pound the end of it square into a wall in front of you. You would use a very simple, powerful motion. You don't want your wrist twisting behind your head, as I mentioned previously, and you don't want it flipping now when you are releasing the ball, either.

I know there are some people who think you should use an exaggerated wrist flip as the ball leaves your hand, kind of an inside-out flip, where your wrist rotates all the way around counter-clockwise (if you're right handed) and your fingers wind up pointing out to the right. John Unitas throws the ball that way, I know, and nobody has thrown the ball any better than John, but it still doesn't make sense to me. He's a genius and he does it, but I'm not sure other people should try to learn that way. I know as soon as I try it, I lose a lot of power. It just feels weak. When I bring my whole body around, I want everything to keep going in the same direction. I don't want to be turning my wrist inside-out and get in the way of all the power I've got.

How can you throw the ball without a wrist flip?

Try this and maybe you'll see

As I release the ball my wrist snaps forward some — not counter-clockwise like many passers — and if I need to get the right arm very high I lean to my left and pull my left arm down.

what I'm saying. Stand normally with your left side about six inches from a wall and your feet spread so you can turn your body to face the wall. Put your right hand up about six inches from your ear as though you had a ball in it and make a fist. Now swing your shoulders around,

release

keeping your fist beside your ear until the last instant, and pound the flat side of your fist into the wall. Watch out you don't knock any mirrors down. The thing isn't worth seven years bad luck.

If you try this, you should see what I'm saying. The easiest, strongest thing to do is also the simplest motion. You just turn all in one piece and wham! you pound the wall. Now imagine yourself doing the same thing but turning your wrist inside-out just as you hit the wall. Don't try it because you might hurt yourself. I think you'll feel the motion gets weak. All that power from your body turn gets lost if your wrist rotates inside out.

When I follow through my arm comes right around and across my body in front of me, following the turn of my body, and my fingers wind up facing out to the left just naturally. There is some snap in my wrist as I let the ball go. The wrist is cocked back just a little as I hold the ball, and as I release the ball my wrist snaps in toward the inside of my forearm. But there is no rotation of the wrist at any time, either behind my head or as I release.

Why is the ball released high?

There are a few things I'm always checking on in my throwing, things that seem to me to be really important in whether I'm throwing well or not. One of these is whether I'm keeping the ball high as I release it.

I don't throw with an exaggerated overhand motion at all. I'm out there with a nice comfortable three-quarters motion, where it doesn't feel like I'm putting too much strain on my shoulder. But I can't get lackadaisical, either, and let my arm start slipping down. Even if I don't throw overhand, I still want to keep on top of the ball any time I have to really get something into the throw.

As my shoulders come around and my arm starts to snap I want that ball to go both forward and up. If I don't reach up as my arm is snapping forward, I don't get an all-out motion. I more push the ball out than snap it out and I don't want that. The idea is to snap the arm up and forward and release the ball at the highest point.

Last summer in training camp I hit a spell where my passes weren't zipping and my arm started to get sore. It wasn't a bad sore arm. I've never had a bad sore arm, sore to where I thought I was doing it damage by throwing. It gets tired sometimes, but not to where I have to lay off it.

I think that's probably because of the way I throw by turning in a circle. There's not much strain on my shoulder and I never really straighten my arm completely as I release, so my elbow is never overextended. Throwing the way I do is easy on the arm.

But at this one point I wasn't throwing well and I was feeling some pain. I had just been thinking about keeping the ball high at the time because I was working on this part of the book, but it's funny sometimes how you won't notice something you're doing until somebody points it out. In this case Kenny Meyer, our backfield coach, told me one day that he thought I was releasing the ball too low. I tried raising my arm and he had it right. My passing improved overnight and the sore arm just disappeared. I had been pushing the ball unnaturally and putting a strain on my elbow.

How do you keep on top of the ball?

As the ball leaves my hand I want the feeling that it's going out nice and high and yet I also want to feel like I'm on top of it, like I have control up and over the ball. I know this sounds like a contradiction, but it works out.

If you take a ball and put it beside your ear and then just go through a slow pushing motion, shoving the ball forward about eye high, you'll see it's hard to keep your hand over on top of the ball much. The natural thing to do with that motion is put your hand under the ball. Now if you put the ball beside your ear and slowly arc the ball up and forward, you'll see you can keep your fingers wrapped around up on top of the ball much easier, even though your hand is high over your head.

I don't overdo getting on top of the ball. I'm not trying to do anything awkward. But I do want that feeling of control, like I'm on top of the situation, anytime I'm throwing with authority.

Picture overleaf: Nothing a passer does about his motion is of any use without a solid cup of pass blockers.

footwork

My idea in footwork is the same as it is in arm action—I don't want much of it. I've got to do enough with my feet to keep my weight together and working for me, but I don't want to be walking all around back there. I want to set up and get that ball out of there. It's all over with in a hurry.

Bad things first, and the worst thing is to take a skip step before throwing. A lot of guys do that. They have a kind of quick right-left forward skip like a shortstop throwing over to first. Some guys on long passes walk into their throw with three steps, left-right-left.

In my opinion that's terrible. If there's anything a quarterback should work on right from the start, it's throwing that ball with one step. If you have to throw it 70 yards, throw it with one step. Hell, sometimes I don't step at all. If a guy has to run up to throw the ball, it just means he hasn't got a good throwing motion.

Why is it bad to take steps?

There are several reasons why stepping up like that is bad. First it takes time. My release, start to finish, takes half a second. I don't have any time to go strolling. Second, it's more motion to get coordinated. It's harder to keep your weight solidly under control if you are moving your feet a lot. But most important, if I skipped forward as I threw I'd just be skipping right into those big cats up in front. Those defensive guys earn their money by charging seven yards to get me. Let them earn it. I'm not going to

walk up to them and make their job easier. The only reason I'll step up is if I'm getting pressure from the outside, from a defensive end. Otherwise, boy, I'm throwing the ball from right here, right where I'm standing.

Why I don't have to take any steps goes back to the way I get set at the end of my dropback. I come to the end of the drop with my weight already forward on my left leg. A guy who stops with his weight on his right leg, his rear leg, has to take a step forward onto his left leg to get his weight going forward. In fact, he usually has to take that little skip step.

But I've already got my weight forward when I come to a stop. I'm leaning in and ready to roll right now.

What is the footwork at the time of the throw?

As I throw, I raise my weight up a little out of that sitting position I've stopped in. As my weight comes up I can step a little with my left leg, if necessary, and then I just whip my body into the turn. It's almost like I take a little jump in place, rather than stepping. My right leg carries the weight at one point, after I straighten up and while I step with my left leg. But I never shift my weight back over that right foot. That would be too much action. I would just have to move the weight forward again as I threw. My right leg carries the weight for a short while but my center of gravity is still forward, between my feet.

What I do with this little jump is to get my weight up and available so I can move it quick, whip those hips and shoulders and get my whole body into it. My

I don't want to waste time getting my weight moving when I want to throw, so as I set up I raise my weight up on my toes— almost jumping some- times—to keep it fluid and ready to whip in a circle.

weight isn't planted heavily down on my feet. If I take that little jump and can't throw yet, sometimes I'll just take another one. The jumps are so small they hardly take any time anyway. Or sometimes I'll just get the weight up once and then keep it up, standing up high on the balls of my feet without actually jumping. But the point is to keep the weight up and fluid and balanced evenly over my two feet, so I don't have to do any work to get myself going.

When I take the jump, my right foot will usually land a little farther back than where it started and my left foot will move a little forward and to the left. I'm not stepping forward, really, I'm just spreading my base a little.

What exactly is the set position to throw?

Another way to say this is I don't want to have to get set to throw. I want to be set, all the time. I don't want to have to take any extra steps or shift my weight around before I throw. I don't drop back and then get set

and then do it. When I come to the end of my dropback, I'm set right then. And I stay set all the time until I unload.

That's the way it has to be. Even when I'm not set, it's almost like I am. I can always deliver the ball. Maybe I get some pressure from one side, or I have to slide around a little to find a throwing lane, but I still try to keep my weight fluid and evenly balanced over my feet so whenever I see somebody to throw to, Boom! it's gone.

Throwing the way I do, I can do this because I don't have to gather my feet and take some steps and get my weight moving from back to front. There's no hard work getting ready to throw. As long as I have my left shoulder closed some, so I can open my body up fast, and as long as I have my weight pretty much over my feet, I can just tip my feet into the ground anywhere down there under me and at the same time have my body already turning. The ball is gone almost as fast as I see the guy.

I don't always actually do this jump. Especially on shorter passes, I go through a whole step that seems more normal. But a jump involving both feet and landing on both feet is much closer to what I'm doing than a right-left forward step, even on those throws where you don't see a jump. My weight goes up, to get fluid, and then it turns. Up and down some, and around in a circle, but not back-to-front too much.

Why is a small step important?

As I say, sometimes I don't even take a step with my left foot, and if I do step I try to take a small one. An overstride is a serious mistake. Now and then Weeb will catch me doing that, stepping out too far and leaving my weight behind. I want to stay in pretty tight and keep that weight on top of the left leg as I go through with the pass. Over-striding is a fault you see a lot, usually with quarterbacks who have their weight back too far to start with. They try to take a big step to pull their weight forward, but it doesn't work and they wind up with their weight kind of stuck in the middle and their legs wide apart. You can't generate any power that way at all.

The step I take with my left leg is usually a little off to the left of where I'm going to throw the ball. But this is more true on passes to my left than on passes to my right. Sometimes throwing to my right I step pretty straight at the target and come over the top more with the throw.

Why does the left toe come up?

One thing is really weird. I never knew this until I looked at our pictures. As I throw the ball, right at the time of maximum power as the ball leaves my hand, the toe of my left foot comes up off the ground. That's weird. My left foot is my front foot. If I were throwing like any other passer, that would be the time when my weight would be all forward and that toe would be driven into the ground hard. But I don't throw this way and nothing shows it better than what my left foot does.

1

2

I have my weight up and ready and then I take a small step and throw almost at the same time, even on a long pass; a big, wide step (above) is one of the worst mistakes I can make.

When I'm at maximum power, the left side of my body is pulling backward as fast as the right side of my body is rolling forward. My body is going in a circle. My left side pulls back so fast that my left leg straightens up some, instead of bending down to take my body weight, and the toe of my left foot gets pulled up off the ground. It's a good thing, too, because when my toe comes up it can turn out to the left some more and allow the rest of my body to keep swinging on around in the circle. If my toe didn't come up and turn out, my cleats would catch as I turned and I might screw my leg off. As a matter of fact, and I don't even like to think about this, on certain types of artificial surfaces even though my toe comes up my foot can't slide around enough and I wind up putting a lot of twist into my left knee. And that knee isn't too good any more anyway.

Just to emphasize speed again, boy, everything that happens with my feet happens quick. I don't push off, then step, then throw. I've got my weight up on my toes and my feet take whatever little step or jump they have to while my shoulders are already starting to open up. It's all right now, Whoom! the ball's gone.

Footwork is vital if I must move around and find a throwing lane.

As I move I keep my weight up on my toes and my legs spread slightly under me.

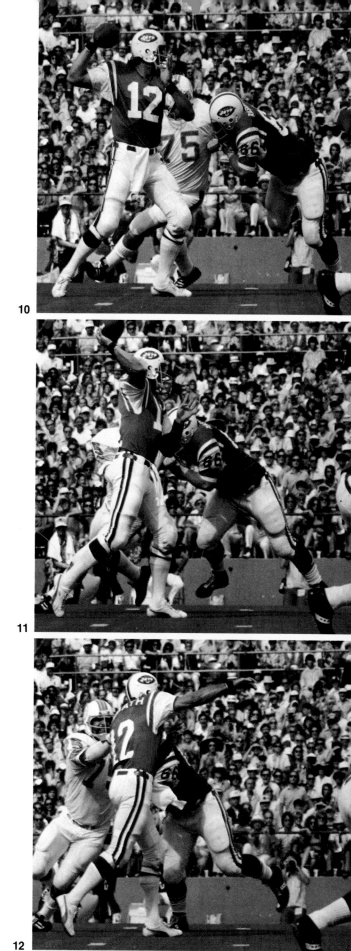

7 10

8 11

9 12

I keep my weight forward and my left shoulder closed and get the ball up.

When I see a receiver the ball goes out as quickly as on any other throw.

late release

This throwing motion has one more advantage. It lets you hold the ball a split second longer and throw the ball with rushers right on you.

A quarterback who has to step up to throw, if he's rushed and can't step up his pass comes out of there weak. He can't get his weight into the throw and that's the kind of pass that gets picked off lots of times. But I don't step up to throw. My weight goes to the left and in a circle and that gives me an extra split second to throw before the rush gets to me. I don't step up into the trouble. I'm throwing right from where I'm standing and that makes those guys come another yard or two to get to me.

My pass also zips out of there just like it does when I'm not rushed. I don't have to change my motion when they're coming at me because I throw this way all the time. Since I know this, I often throw the ball in pressure that would cause some quarterbacks to pull it down and eat it. Of course, I probably also throw some interceptions when I should have eaten the ball.

Since I throw without moving forward much I can throw the ball quite late. Sometimes I get hit afterward but I'm going to get hit anyway so the ball might as well be gone.

1

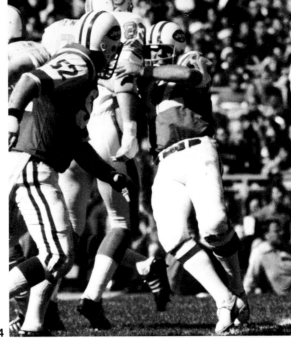

4

2

5

3

6

survival

There's a bonus that comes with using a body turn to throw the ball. Maybe the reason to get into throwing like this is because it's easier and quicker, but after you do it awhile you find out it has an extra advantage. It helps keep you from getting killed after you've thrown the ball.

Most guys passing step up into their throw. They step forward right into the rush that is coming at them. That means they are throwing their weight into a collision. Quarterbacks are always getting nailed just after they throw the ball and most of them make it tough on themselves because they have their momentum going forward and they smash headlong into the big guys charging in at them. No quarterback ever hurt a defensive tackle this way.

How does the body turn help in a collision?

When I throw, things are completely different. I hardly ever step up into those guys. I step out to the side a little and turn around. Instead of moving forward, my weight is moving to the left and then on around and away from the line. I can take the blow a lot easier because my body is already moving away naturally and when a guy hits

Since I'm turning around as I throw I'm usually turning away from a collision instead of stepping right into it.

me, I'm just flying anyway. It's a lot better than stepping up in there and really getting popped. At least my 200 pounds isn't going up against the other guy's 270 or whatever. My 200 pounds is working with his, and things don't usually get so bad. Sometimes I'll be coming on around and some guy will put one on me pretty good but it just knocks me farther back. I come running out of the pocket like a pussy cat getting away from a pack of dogs.

Is this escape mechanism a conscious thing?

At one point in time, I thought about this a lot, about getting away from the big hits. This was after I came up to the pros. There were some times when maybe I wasn't throwing that well out to my left and Weeb was telling me that I was opening up too much as I threw, turning my body too much and affecting my throw. Now sometimes I do open up too much, get my left side turned all the way around before I'm ready to throw and I wind up just flipping the ball out there with my arm. But that doesn't mean the turn is bad in itself, just turning too early.

I thought about it and decided I definitely want to be going away when I'm hit. What the hell. Why ask to get killed? Looking back on my career I know I've only been hurt throwing once. I played five pro years without missing a game before I broke my wrist. The next summer I hurt my knee trying to make a tackle. That was a fluke and I went through all last season again without getting hurt, hurt to where I couldn't play. And

Whenever I can I keep on turning and fall on my hands and arms, and sometimes my momentum takes me running out of the hit altogether like a cat escaping a pack of dogs.

you have to remember I'm not a scrambler. You know I'm not running out of any trouble, so I must know something about getting hit and falling. I think I do.

How do you fall after getting hit?

If I have got around in my turn before I get hit, then I keep on going around and break my fall with my hands. But I can't always do that. Throwing out to my right especially, I don't always get turned before I'm hit. There just isn't as much body turn when I'm throwing to my right. So sometimes I'll take a shot head-on from my right side and then I'll try to go with the blow—roll with the punches so to speak.

The thing I really try to avoid is falling on my side. There's something about getting hit over on your side with some big dude on top of you that really hurts. Your body can't give through your shoulders and you can get a shoulder injury or snap your collarbone or something. If I get hung up going down on my side, I always try to roll with it, have my weight coming on over instead of falling straight down on my shoulder.

1

2

3

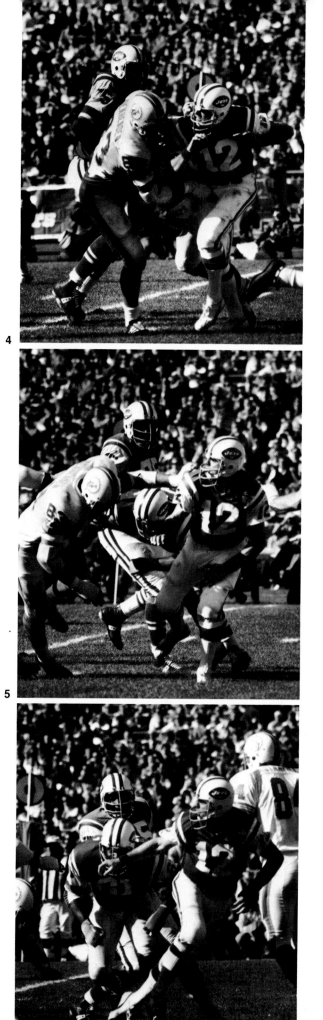

4

5

6

body and mind

Getting yourself together physically is only part of becoming a good passer. You've got to have a good motion in order to have much chance out there at all, but just a good motion doesn't make a good passer. It's not only in the arm. It's also in the head.

A good quarterback has to know what kind of pass to throw in each situation, when to throw it and why. He also has to know when *not* to throw that ball, when to throw it away where it won't do any harm, even when to eat the ball if that's the best choice available. And in order to know these things, a quarterback must first know himself. What can I throw? What *can't* I throw? What are my capabilities?

Why is it important to know your own capabilities?

If I don't know what kind of passes I can throw and what I can't, I'm going to get myself in all kinds of trouble. There's not much room out there and if I want to put a ball in a hole I better know that I can do it. It doesn't do any good to fool myself. They'll just keep running the ball back at me.

On long passes, for instance, everybody has a range. If a quarterback is standing here and his receiver starts running

When I start moving around in the pocket, I have to know my throwing capabilities. If I keep on going out to my left and throw back to my right, like I do here to Eddie Bell, I have to know I can get the ball there on time.

Usually there are fewer defensive players near the sidelines and it's safer to throw there. But if they double cover out wide, a receiver like Richard Caster has to find an open spot in the middle.

straight out, there comes a point in time for everybody when the ball is just not going to get there. Every quarterback has to know where that point is for himself. Say I go back and look left and that's no good, then I check the center and it's busy, by the time I come around to my right my receiver on that side may be out there long *long*. Too far. I've got to know this right now and not even try it. Find someplace to dump the ball off and avoid the loss. And when I say the guy's out too far, I mean he's out too far to throw the ball by taking one step and throwing as if I were throwing a hook pass. There's no time out there to be winding up and running three or four steps to throw the ball. I have to be able to throw quick because I never know when I'm going to go long. I may come around, see the guy, and fly it right now. So when I say I have to know how far I can throw, I mean how far I can throw right now with one step.

Or say I'm getting some heat and I'm moving out of my pocket out to the left. Maybe I'll see somebody open back to my right side and 20 yards deep. Now that's an awkward throw, moving left and throwing right. If I'm going to try it I better damn sure know I can get the ball there in good shape, and if I can't I just have to find something else.

How can you adjust to your capabilities?

If a guy is out of your range, there's not much you can do. But sometimes you can catch yourself forcing other kinds of passes and find a way to help yourself. Like last year in mid-season, all of a sudden I found that when I was throwing a sideline pass about 20 yards deep, the damn ball was get-ting there low all the time. It was bouncing on the ground. On a deep sideline pass like that, the ball is in the air a long way. My receiver is 20 yards down-field, I'm 7 or 8 back, and there's maybe 25 yards between me and the sideline. The ball can easily be traveling 35 or 40 yards to get there. What I figured out was that I was trying to throw the ball too flat. I was trying to line it out there as if the guy was running a slant over the middle.

As soon as I figured that, I raised my release a little and put a little more arc on the ball. The ball got there in good shape and I just threw it a bit earlier in order to keep the timing the same, so the ball would be there when my receiver turned around.

Is it possible to throw the ball too hard?

Most of that stuff you hear about guys throwing the ball too hard, that's all nonsense. The harder you throw, the faster you get the ball where it's sup-posed to be, the less time the defense has to react.

Of course, this doesn't mean every pass you throw, you get on it all out. Throwing swings out in the flat to your backs you can lighten up a little because the back is at sort of an awkward angle and usually there's no defender right on him. Some-times throwing over the center to your backs, or on a slant to a wide receiver, you'll take a little off, too. The ball may only go 10 or 15 yards in the air and that can be a tough pass to handle if you throw it full speed. If you try to gun it, you better hit that guy right in the chest. It's a tough hand catch.

But even over center, I don't throw any passes you'd call soft. There's a lot of defensive people ganged up in the middle and even if my guy is open I want to line him the ball before some company shows up.

Is it safer throwing to the side-lines or over the middle?

I've heard some quarterbacks say they would rather throw over the middle than out wide. Their reasoning is that a pass over the center is a shorter throw, an easier throw, and that if a side-line pass falls a little short and the defensive back gets it, that's a quick six for the wrong team.

I can understand this thinking, but I don't agree with it. Of course I don't have any problem throwing the sideline pass and so maybe that's part of it. If it's hard for you to throw that pass straight with enough on it, then maybe it *is* too dangerous.

But for me, the middle is the most dangerous place to throw the ball. There are just so many people in there.

That's why I almost always zip the ball pretty good when I'm throwing over center. If I can see the guy is open right now, I want to get him the ball right now before something can happen. It helps him, too, to get the ball quicker. Then he can get himself moving before he gets sandwiched between two or three guys.

What if you can't see your receiver?

It's tough to see out there. Those are big people in front of you, five of your own guys and at least four of theirs. There aren't many cracks to see through and if you're having trouble you have to lean your body this way and that way and get up on your toes and just get into a peek-a-boo thing until you find somebody.

Sometimes I don't even see my receiver. I don't say that happens often, but now and then I throw without seeing the guy. It's not a recommended thing to do, but if I know where the defense is, I'll take the chance. I don't do it over the middle—that's just too dangerous —but on deep sideline passes where I know where the receiver is supposed to be I'll go ahead and throw it blind.

How important is timing in throwing the ball?

Passes to the tight end aren't usually timed up too closely. He has to wade out through a lot of traffic. The strong side line-

Picture overleaf: Sometimes nothing is working right and then you just have to pull it down and get moving.

backer bumps him and then maybe the middle linebacker or the safety takes a crack at him and he has to sort of just feel his way around out there and find himself an open spot. I can't throw that ball on timing, because I never know how long it's going to take him to get somewhere. It depends on how many bodies he has to hassle. I just have to wait until he gets someplace alone and then get him the ball.

Throwing to the wide receivers, sometimes the timing is more important. On any kind of side-line pass, that ball better be there when he comes out of his move. The defensive back has a good angle and if the ball is late at all, he's going to step in and take it right home.

Throwing an inside move to a wide receiver can be different. On that one, your receiver gets in between you and the defensive back and screens him off the play. The ball doesn't have to be there quite as quick. A lot of times, your receiver starts coming in and you can wait and hit him anywhere you want over the center. And we've got in trouble trying to throw that inside pass perfectly. Maybe I throw the ball while my receiver's back is still turned, expecting him to cut in. The defensive back sees the ball and starts to move up and my receiver looks at the guy coming up and doesn't know why. He doesn't see the ball with his back turned and he thinks he can just break his pattern and go by the guy deep. Boom! The ball hits the defensive back right in the chest. That's happened. I've experienced that.

So trying to time up an inside move isn't always the best idea.

When can an underthrow be a good throw?

A passer not only has to be able to throw straight, he has to have a feel in his head in order to hit a guy who may catch the ball 60 or 70 yards away moving at top speed.

One way to get out of the problem is just to throw a pass short. That might not sound very smart, but every now and then it works out. I can send my wide receiver racing down the side-lines and then deliberately throw a poor pass, throw it short, and let the receiver slow up under it and make the catch. Against certain cornerbacks, especially guys who play bump-and-run, this can work nice because the cornerman is trailing my guy a little bit and running all out and he doesn't have a chance to look up for the ball. The ball drops in there short and the receiver can see it and stops quick and the cornerman just keeps on going.

We got into this by accident, just having it happen to us a couple of times, and seeing that maybe we were onto a good thing. You can't really do it too much, but if we see a chance, see a guy who keeps his head turned, we'll try it. We did it twice in a row a couple of years ago. We were behind the Raiders a few points late in the game and backed up to our own goal line. Don Maynard went out there and I underthrew him and he stopped

and got it about the 50 and on the next play we did it again and this time he caught the ball and stepped around the cornerback and scored. Maybe it doesn't look too pretty from the stands, but I kinda like the way it looks on the scoreboard.

How do you throw a long pass?

Not every long pass is the same. Sometimes I want to line the ball out there pretty good and sometimes it's better to put some loft on it.

If my man is going down the sidelines and a safety is trying to get over there from the inside, I want to line that ball out there, get it there before the safety can get over. But if the man is being chased from behind by the cornerman, I loft it, put it up over the guy. Another time I'll line it as if the receiver is running a deep slant between two guys who are playing zone, running right down the seam between the zones. I want the ball to get there before the guys can pinch in and get there.

There's another time when throwing a bad pass is throwing a good pass. That's when you've got nobody open and you've got company back there in the pocket and you've got to do something quick or it's going to be third and 17. What you do is throw the ball away. Throw a "bad" pass and miss everybody. Of course, you throw it well enough that a referee isn't going to have to call you for grounding. He can't stand there in front of 60,000 people and let you throw the ball 40 yards into the stands. But if you pay attention to what you're doing, you should be able to play that ball "safe," like we

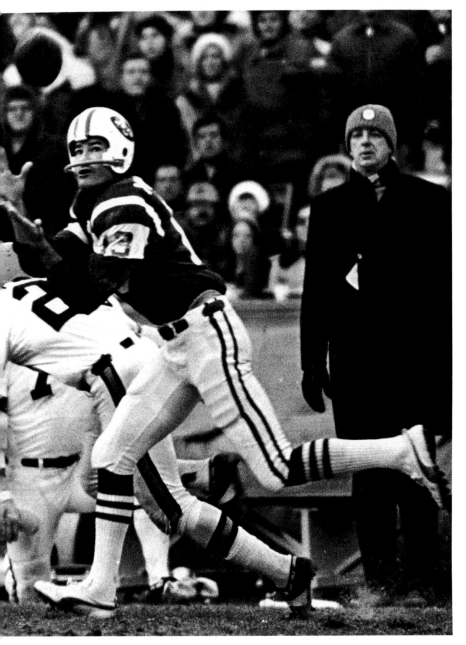

This pass fell a little short and to the inside. Don Maynard adjusted but the defensive back got lost, as sometimes happens on an underthrow, and the play went for a 72-yard touchdown.

say in pool, put it where it doesn't do you much good but it doesn't do the other team any good either.

Where can you throw the ball away?

The safest place to unload the ball is out of bounds, of course, because it doesn't matter who catches the ball out there, it's just exercise. On a lot of pass patterns your last receiver, your outlet man, is over near the sidelines. He's usually a back running a swing or a wide receiver on an out pattern. If you are forced to come around to him and he's not open either and the heat's on, you just lift the ball up a little and get it off the field.

But sometimes you get trapped looking over the center, ready to throw in there, and the crunch is coming too quick to readjust yourself to throw out of bounds. You're stuck trying to throw the ball away over the center, but you'd better be careful in there, boy. There's a lot of people in the middle and you better know where you're putting the ball.

First off, over the center, it's not too wise to overthrow your man. The ball may clear him and the guy guarding him, but there's always a safety or two running around out there deep and you might miss everybody in the short zones and hit one of those safeties right in the hands. Throwing away over the middle it's safer to try to miss the people you are looking at to the side a little bit and zip the ball low. Even then you have to be sure there aren't any spare linebackers running around. Have everybody accounted for who might make the play.

ball handling

Ball handling is really a pretty simple part of the job. My goal is simply to get the ball to the runner cleanly every time. I know I do some things about the handoff and fake handoff different than other quarterbacks, but I have my reasons. What I'm doing makes sense to me.

When I get the ball from center, the first thing I do is pull it back into my stomach. This is a simple thing, but it's important for a couple of reasons. In the first place, I'm trying to keep the ball hidden from the other team, and if it's tucked away in my belly, it's harder to see. Second, I don't want that ball waving around out where it could get knocked away. There's a lot of traffic back there—backs are crossing and guards are pulling, and a lot of people on defense are trying to jump in there, too. So I pull that ball back in safe next to my body.

How do you use your feet?

You have to get your footwork settled for every play, but all it takes is a little practice. The idea is that I want to end up close enough to my runner so I don't have to go stretching out after him. But I don't want to crowd the guy either, and maybe run him off course.

The thing I try to keep in mind in general is this: Don't overstep yourself. Don't reach way out with one foot to where you lose control of your weight. Say you're going right down the line for a quick dive handoff over

right tackle. When you take that first lead step with your right foot, only make it about 12 inches or so. Otherwise you'll get your leg out in front of your weight and you'll get off balance. Or let's say you have to do a reverse pivot, turn all the way around clockwise to your right and wind up handing off on a play over left tackle. Don't lead out and around with your right foot and take a big step. I try to do it the same way I drop back to pass—I sit down into the turn, keep my rear end low, and throw that right side back and around. I pull my right elbow and hip around, and keep sitting down low, and my right foot just naturally comes out about where it's supposed to be. This is the kind of move you should practice over and over to where it comes naturally in a game.

The specific things about footwork you'll have to work out for each play with your coaches and backs. But the goal is just to practice it enough so that it's natural and relaxed.

What is the handoff technique?

If your feet have got you in the right place to make the handoff, all you have to do is set the ball in against the runner's belly as he goes by. I just lay the ball in there softly, like it's an egg. I want the exchange to be as smooth and easy as possible.

I know some quarterbacks like to whap the ball against the runner's stomach—really pop it, make it "solid." But I don't think this makes much sense. I don't want to make the runner's job any harder than it is. I don't want him flinching or looking down to see when the ball is going to hit him. He has to be

> **To start every handoff, I pull the ball back into my stomach to protect it, sit backward a little and yank my side around.**

watching up front, looking for his hole. I don't want him to have to pay any attention to the handoff at all. He should just find himself in the hole with the ball under his arm.

Besides, if I'm swinging my arm to slap the ball in there, I'm making my job tougher. Swinging my arm like that is excess motion and it makes for a greater margin for error. Now and then an unnecessary move causes me to miss the spot a little and the runner has to be grabbing for the ball instead of making a cut. Worse yet, I could wind up with the ball rolling around on the ground. I don't want to make any extra problems for myself. I just take the ball and lay it in there soft, like a little old egg.

How important is faking?

On handoffs it is the quarterback's responsibility to get the ball to the ball carrier. On fake handoffs it is the halfback or fullback who has the greater responsibility for making a good fake.

Some other quarterbacks make more out of faking than I do. They go through more deliberate motions. They fake going back to pass or rolling out after the handoff and things like that. There's some good reasons why they do it, and I've been working lately on carrying out my fakes

I lay the ball in softly, trail my hand out after the runner and try to keep the other hand in where it might have the ball concealed if the play were a fake. On a rare front hand-off (right) I just try to skip back out of the way.

more on certain types of plays.

But I've got some reasons for doing it my way, too. First off, in the pros, nobody on defense pays much attention to the quarterback, anyway. He can go through all the fakes he wants, but the guys on defense are watching their keys, they aren't looking at him. They watch where the guards go, what the backs do, and so on. They don't pay a lot of attention to the ball because it's easy for the backfield to hide the ball. The ball's only a foot long or something. It can get lost pretty easy. But guards are more than six feet tall. You can't lose them, and they have to go and block where the runner is going to go, most of the time. So defensive people watch the blockers and backs a lot more than they watch the quarterback.

Now, that's in the pros. In high school, sometimes, guys still watch the ball and faking can be more important. I know on my high school team our coach, Larry Bruno, was a fiend for faking. We had the fakingest team anybody ever saw. Even referees used to tell us they had never seen anybody handle the ball like we did. So in high school, maybe, faking can mean more.

But there's another reason why I don't turn my back after a

handoff and drop back or roll out. I want to see what's going on. If I turn my back and keep on faking I can't see what happens— if the blockers go right, or if some defensive back is coming up too fast.

What happens when you keep the ball?

Say I fake a handoff and want to pass. Where do I want to be looking? Downfield, of course, so I can read the pass coverage. That's why when I keep the ball I do the same thing I do on a handoff. I trail my free hand out after the fake and look back over my shoulder as though I'm following the runner. Actually I'm looking downfield, but the thing is, I look just the same as I do on a handoff. I just take it really casual and hide the ball away in my stomach or down behind my hip or wherever is best for that particular play. I don't draw any attention to myself when I keep the ball. I always look the same, and that's all that matters.

I think this way of doing it makes sense most of the time. Take a draw play, for instance. If those defensive linemen haven't rushed themselves into a bad position while I'm dropping back on the fake pass, it's too late by the time I give the ball to the runner. There's nothing I can do by keeping up the fake of a pass. If there's a hole, thank goodness. If not, it's second and 15. There's nothing I can do by carrying out the fake except miss seeing what happens.

Of course, everything a quarterback does depends on the situation he is in. Sometimes faking really makes a difference. You just have to know when to get into it.

On a fake handoff, I do the same as on a handoff — I trail my hand out, look over the shoulder as though I'm watching the runner and hide the ball away casually. The move shown here is especially tough because I have to turn so far around to get set to throw.

There was a time in the preseason game against Dallas last year when we were on the one-yard line with only time for one more play in the half. We had been down on the one once before and that time we scored by faking to the fullback straight ahead and giving to the halfback off-tackle. This time I thought we could run the same play but get the ball right in there quick by giving to the fullback. Now that's a time you better believe I went on and carried out a good fake to the halfback. He did a great job of faking too, and our fullback popped into the end zone before anybody on the defense could react. We saw films on it later and it was great. We didn't have a man to block one of their linebackers, but the fake just froze that man. He started in, then out, then in, then out. He never got off his spot. A time like that, faking makes a big difference.

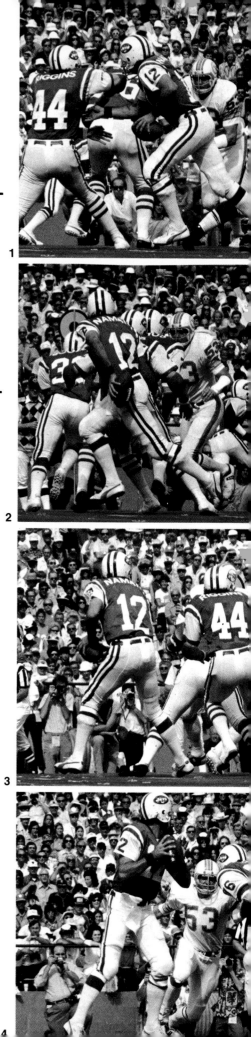

CHECKLIST

Joe covered a lot of material on throwing in this section. In order to sum up and be of some assistance to quarterbacks who would like to deliver a football this way, we are including a series of checklist questions here, along with some hints to follow if any particular aspect of the style seems to be particularly troublesome.

Let me say this in front. Namath's style can be learned. I know because I learned it, and I did so without the benefit of all the photographs and the details of Joe's thinking on each topic. It's a throwing style that is simple and physically efficient. But I should also say it isn't a style you pick right up. You can't get away from years of a less effective way of throwing in a few hours or days. Unless you are a rare exception, your motion is probably considerably different from the one described here. A good way to approach the problem would be to wait until the off-season and then spend the spring and early summer getting yourself into it. Start by just placing the ball up beside your head, cocking your left shoulder around in front of your chin and then wheeling around and pounding the ball out. Be sure to reach high with your arm as you release the ball.

After you're locked in on the basic turning rhythm, begin putting the other details around it. As it starts to come together, you ought to feel the power of it; and a lot of the detail Joe points out will probably just happen automatically.

People read books in order to learn a golf swing and after some practice they can do it. There's no reason why you can't read a book and learn a passing motion, especially an easy one that uses many of the same principles of a golf swing or a hitter's swing. Practice hard, but have fun. You may not get to throw as well as Joe, but if learning his style does as much for you as it did for me, the enjoyment of zipping those sideline passes under pressure will more than make up for the work you had to do to get your motion together.

1. Do you feel sluggish getting away from center?
Sit down into the turn. Yank your right side back and around. Explode away with a false step by your right foot. Push off strongly with the left leg. Sprint back full steam.

2. Is your weight back and hard to move at the end of the dropback?
Stop your dropback with your weight over your forward foot, then straighten up. Never put your main weight over the rear foot.

3. Do you have trouble getting your turn started quickly?
After stopping the dropback, raise up on the balls of your feet. Center your weight over both feet.

4. Are you having trouble getting power into your turn?
Be sure to get your left side cocked all the way around to the right with your left shoulder under your chin. Then uncoil as you throw.

5. Is the ball getting behind your turn and coming through late?
Keep the ball up chest high as you set up. Don't bounce it up and down or arc it in a circle as you start to raise it. Bring it straight up.

6. Is your turn getting locked and choking your throwing motion?
Be sure to step out to your left a little, not right at the target, so your body can turn all the way around.

7. Are you having trouble getting your weight up and around on your left leg?
Don't overstride. Keep the step with the left foot small so your weight stays on top of it.

8. Does the turn seem to be dislocated, in different stages?
Whip the whole body around as one piece—hips, left arm and shoulders.

9. Does the left arm seem to be flopping loosely?
Keep the left arm bent at the elbow. Keep the arm solid as it whips around and down. Keep the arm and the shoulders solid and turning together.

10. Does the throwing arm seem to flip or wave or become disconnected from the turn?
Bring the arm straight up and out. Don't bring it backward to cock it. Get it up near the head and then slam it forward. Keep your wrist closed so the ball seems to point down the throwing line at all times.

11. Do you seem to be pushing the ball? Does your throw lack snap?
Snap your arm upward as you slam it forward. Release the ball high.

12. Are you having trouble getting on top of the ball and really powering it?
Pull your left shoulder down and your right shoulder up and reach up on top as you slam your shoulders around.

13. Do you follow through in the direction of your throw?
Pull the left side of your body back as fast as the right side goes forward. Spin on your left heel and follow through to the left and away from the line.

4 game day

It's Sunday. Game day. The cavernous horseshoe tiers of Shea Stadium's open-ended stands will fill today and 60,000 people will watch Namath and the Jets do for real what they have practiced all week in private.

"I feel good, boy," he says as we walk under the stands to the locker room. "I feel fast. I may just do some running out there today."

We're both laughing and he kicks the locker room door open. "Aww Ri-i-ite!" he hollers walking in. "Ready to *roll!*"

It is two hours to kickoff and there are only two other players in the room. The equipment man, Bill Hampton, is sitting on one side. "What happened, Joe? he says. "You fall out of bed?"

"I'm ready to roll," Joe answers. "What's with this radio?" He gets up on a stool and fiddles with the big radio that sets the mood in the room. Musak strings disappear and the Allman Brothers band is soon laying out a rolling, driving beat. "Aww Rite."

The room begins to fill with big men in various states of undress. Joe wanders for awhile, joking some, making multiple trips to the john. Finally he strips down and then dresses back as far as his shorts. He pulls out his knee braces and sits down in front of his locker. "Damn," he says, holding the braces in each hand and inspecting them casually. He tapes

the simple one—the one that is only a small hinge and two short bars—on the outside of his right knee. Then he just sits. He picks up a copy of the game program, leafs through it, and puts it down. He picks up the complex brace for his left knee, an amazing contraption of bent metal and slabs of stretch elastic. Then he puts it down. He raps with some of the players and a couple of visitors. He signs a few autographs.

"I don't want to put this thing on," he says. "I don't. It's a pain." But violent collisions are waiting outside the door. Finally, slowly, he lays the brace in position, wraps the elastic around and tapes it in position. The frail, famous knees have asserted their dominance again.

A team's final preparation for a football game is a private matter, and after the Jets return from their pre-game warmups I go out on the field to take in the marching bands and strutting girls.

And then, behind the gate that is behind one goal post, milling and bumping and clapping and shouting, the players appear for introductions like bulls waiting in the chute. "At left end, wearing number 83..." and the players emerge one by one, packing their bulky awkward pads, each running out his personality in front of the assembled attention —prancing or slogging or rushing or gliding.

The full squads come crunching out and now time seems to telescope, to fold up on top of itself. The last hour has been a pleasant pageant, but reality is about to change. Namath and three other players meet at midfield and shake hands. The

band plays the National Anthem. Suddenly the ball is high in the air, pinwheeling wildly, and two lines of human beings rush together crashing in the super-reality of body slammed against body.

Namath shuffles out into the contact area, head down, snapping his chin strap. He kneels quickly in the huddle and then the Jets clap their way out and up to the line. Joe folds down over the center's back. His body bobs and sways as he looks back over his shoulder, turns to holler numbers and colors each way and crack! John Riggins is busting straight ahead for eight yards. The team huddles up again and comes out to the line. The lines charge, Emerson Boozer slants outside for five yards, and the scene of battle starts to slide away downfield, big men pounding at each other for the right to symbolic possession of yardage on a white-lined field.

The frantic struggle is strangely soundless, muffled under the background noise from the crowd. Even when there is no cheering, as Joe hollers his signals out at the line, the commanding voice that rings throughout the stadium at practice now comes to the sideline thin and distant.

The crowd throws out its first big roar as Joe fades back to pass but the ball slices untouched out

(continued)

"I don't like that feeling, walking up and down the sidelines before the first play. The adrenalin is flowing and my body is acting up on me. And the feeling lasts even after I go on the field and into the huddle."

"When I get up over center, it's all business then. There's no time to be nervous because my mind is working on the problem at hand, checking the linebackers and the rest of the defense. It's a long ways from the sidelines to the line of scrimmage."

"A football field is a busy place. Besides doing the thinking I've got to be sure on my handoffs, read pass coverages, find myself a place to throw, deliver the ball straight, and handle getting hit afterward. It's an afternoon's work."

"The crowd doesn't affect me. I even try to use the fans' excitement to psyche myself up sometimes when I'm on the sidelines, but it doesn't work. There's too much thinking to do and too much talking with coaches and other players to pay any attention to the crowd."

"There's times to be passive and times to be active.
When somebody grabs my face mask, I just go with it.
I'm not fighting anybody who's pulling me around
by the mask. But if a referee blows a call, I think
I ought to take some action. I don't think I should just
stand around if they're hurting my team."

"It's fun when it's really working. The blockers are doing their job, I'm reading the defense right, the receivers are finding the open spots. It feels crisp and brisk. We're rolling."

One of the best feelings I know is coming off the field after scoring a touchdown and winning a game. You did the studying and practicing, you went out and accomplished what you set out to do, and walking across the field afterward there's just a good feeling going on inside.

GAME DAY (continued)

of bounds. There's a punt and then a cracking explosion of sound shocks the stadium. Fumble! Jets' ball. The offense hustles out and Riggins pounds across in two shots.

As the game goes on, the strange dichotomy between pageant and battle begins to dissolve in the insistent reality of elemental struggle. Uniforms begin to bag, unwind, disappear under smears of turf. The bench fills with men gasping for breath and grabbing at oxygen and Gatorade. Finely tuned athletes come limping out of the action, staggering out with eyes seeking blindly, walking out slowly with one arm hanging dead.

And in the center of the action is Namath, dragging his two legs like dead weights, transformed as he steps up behind the center from his usual easy moving calm into a flashing, spinning, fast-striking high. Every move is quick and finely carved. There is a genius inside him, working through him, and everybody in the stadium pays his respects to it with enthusiastic attention.

Genius isn't always enough in a sport as demanding as football. One of Namath's passes falls short, into the wrong arms, and Joe walks off slowly with his head down, not eager to face the immediate questions he will get from Weeb Ewback. But in a few minutes he is out there again, struggling desperately away from a blitz as Emerson Boozer materializes twenty yards open in the end zone. A last gasp pass

barely flutters in safely and Joe comes racing down to grab Boozer, slap his hat, and trot laughing off the field.

A football game is an emotional roller coaster. From the tense moments in sideline discussion through the frantic physical activity on the field, from the screaming matches with recalcitrant referees through the quiet hand-slap of a teammate's congratulation, Namath's afternoon passes in a flickering succession of changing emotions.

This game will be a win for the Jets, a big win on a day when they can't afford to lose, and the fourth quarter is a display of athletic excellence exercised for its own sake. The gun goes off, and the team files through the small door, down a corridor and into the steaming happiness of a winning dressing room. Only Namath remains behind on the field for one last obligation—an interview on network television.

The win is officially blessed today with some big name visitors. Harry Belafonte stops by and the premier of Nova Scotia says hello and then Henry Kissinger comes in, carrying on the football tradition of his boss in Washington. Namath says, "How are you doing? We had your gatefold picture up in here, I want you to know that." He's talking about the trick photograph of Kissinger stretched out nude a la Burt Reynolds that the Harvard Lampoon ran in a parody of Cosmopolitan. "We had it right over there on the bulletin board, but I guess one of the coaches tore it down."

And as Joe and his teammates live the happiness of victory in the glow of man-made light

under the stands, up above the evening grey settles and thickens in the stadium, cushioning the final scenes of game day. A few children and a few guards play well-defined roles in a game of chase and holler, using the same field the pros had occupied not long before. Individual sounds are back and the Whup! of wooden chairs folded in a far corner echoes thickly from the black hollows in the stands. High above, with the field lights shining weirdly off their peaks, white birds wheel and turn and flow together.

And then the lights wink off, row after row, and the stadium settles in for the barren night, deserted by the athletes who performed with grace and power, deserted by the audience that responded with emotion and involvement, waiting inert for a new influx of energy on another game day.

It is nearly two hours after the final gun when Joe walks out of the stadium. Only a few fans have waited patiently for his appearance and he talks with them briefly as he moves across the parking lot. Then, with the slow, careful movements of a bruised body, he folds into a big car with some friends and moves away into the rest of his life.

5 a quarterback's mind

Playing quarterback, Joe Namath has to think as well as act. Football is so complicated that coaches use computers to help them organize their strategic ideas, and when the game begins it is the quarterback who has to carry the main burden of bringing those ideas to life.

Given my personal Sunday afternoon avocation, no part of my discussion with Joe was more interesting or immediately useful than his thoughts on the quarterback's role as strategic leader. He has the reputation around the NFL as a first-rate field leader, a man who can impose his personality on the shape of the game. Different experts single out different facets of his style for special comment—including his use of audibles, his grasp of the passing game and his rapport with his teammates—and as we talked together I began to see that his reputation has a solid basis. Not only that, I began to put some of his thinking to use

right away and the results were extremely gratifying.

Even semi-pro quarterbacks can upgrade their play-calling if they pay attention to the conceptions of a dedicated professional.

As Joe said repeatedly during our discussions, his ideas aren't the only right ones and they certainly aren't all original. He has had a sound coaching background. His coach in high school was Larry Bruno, and despite the fact that Bruno replaced him at quarterback halfway through his junior year, exiling him to halfback until his senior season, Namath respects him considerably. And his coach at Alabama, Paul "Bear" Bryant, is one of the outstanding coaches at the college level. By the time Namath reached the pros, he already had

advanced knowledge about reading defenses and reacting quickly to the situation as it confronted him. In the pros, his head coach has been Weeb Ewbank, the only coach who ever won championships in both the National Football League and the since-merged American Football League, and the only coach who has ever helped train two quarterbacks of the calibre of John Unitas and Joe Namath.

Given this background and his own extensive experience, Namath has an approach to the game which is detailed and consistent. Much of his thinking —on such topics as leadership, reading defenses and getting the mind "in shape"—covers areas not often included in published discussions of football. Quarterbacks haven't usually been anxious to discuss their thinking in terms that are so easily understood.

responsibility

Playing quarterback, a guy has to like to carry responsibility. It's the kind of job that can make you a little concerned, a little nervous. Even though you know your job, you think, "Doggone, now. I've got to do this thing right."

Think about it for a minute, all the things I have a chance to do wrong playing quarterback. First I can call the wrong play, a play that isn't any good in our situation or against the defense we are facing. Another thing would be to try to make us run a play out of a formation where it's impossible. That's embarrassing. I've done that.

Or I can mess up by calling the play in the wrong tone of voice, using the wrong manner. If you're not sure of yourself, of what you're doing, hell, those other guys are going to pick it right up.

Then I can get up to the line and find I put the formation into the sidelines. Maybe I've called an end run but I've called it to the side where the sideline is closest. Of course, this isn't as big a problem now that the hashmarks have been squeezed together and there's more room to the closer sideline. But it's still a problem to some degree, it still makes a difference on certain plays.

Next, I can look at their defense and see they've got my play covered but then remember that I have a quick snap count and I haven't got time to call an audible and change the play. I'm locked in because as soon as I open my mouth the team is going to run the play I've got called, a bad play.

Or I can look out and see a weakness in the defense but not have my mind moving fast enough to think of the right play and call it there at the line. I can be a little lazy mentally and just let things slide by, going with the play I've got.

It's even possible to forget the snap count. I've done that a few times. I'm looking here at the defense, then over there, trying to think if I should change the play, keeping in mind what I have to do on the play I already called and, hell! What's the count? One or two? I forgot. All I can do is wait for the snap and react and hope I can get into my move fast enough to get the play off.

And then, of course, once I get the ball in my hands it's a whole new ball game. If it's a pass play I have to look out and try to see what the pass defense is doing and then when I figure that out, I have to remember which of my five receivers is likely to come open against that particular defense. And then after all this is over, I have to throw the ball on target.

How should a quarterback approach his mental responsibilities?

My overall idea about how to handle the mental parts of the game is this: do your thinking beforehand. I haven't got the time on the field to do much abstract thinking about how to approach the game of football.

At one point in time I've thought about it and the coaches have thought about it and we have decided what types of things we want to do in any given situation against any given defense. But out there on the field, I'm not thinking up new plays too often. What I'm doing is reacting. A situation registers in my mind and even before I have to think about it I'm already reacting the way I want.

How important is experience?

Being able to react like this is something that comes with experience, being in situations over and over, being familiar with problems that come up because they've come up before and you remember them. It's a question of having good retention. I feel I'm fortunate because where football is concerned I've always had good retention. I can remember things that have happened and use the experience to my advantage. Talking about going to school, taking a biology class or something, I never really had all that good retention because I just wasn't interested in biology. Even if I tried to psyche myself up, studying for exams just didn't turn me on. I know school work is super important, but I wasn't mature enough at the time I was going to school to realize how important. Any of you kids who are still in school and still have most of life in front of you, you should study like crazy to help yourself get ready for the years to come. It's a lot more fun doing things when you have confidence you can do them in style.

Today I'm sorry I hadn't figured it out about school. But football has always been another matter. When I get over center and start scanning the defense, man, every part of me is alive. I'm up, I'm on, my mind is going full speed. And when that's happening I have good retention. And it all adds up over a career. I don't get surprised much in a football game any more. Once in a while, but not often.

What if you don't have experience?

You don't have to wait until you're a ten-year pro to start making plans. You don't have to be third and goal on the other team's eight before you think about what you would want to do if you *were* third and goal on the other team's eight. You can think about these things in advance. You can decide what your general approach will be in most situations you will ever face. That doesn't mean you can completely pre-plan what you will do. Maybe their cornerman gets hurt and you want to go against his replacement as soon as you see him.

But the more thinking you do ahead of time, the easier it's going to be. And I know the easier I can make it on myself when I'm on the field, the more I like it. There's a lot of responsibility and a lot of ways to screw up. Playing football or in any other part of life, I want to cut down my margin for error as much as I can ahead of time.

Planning ahead with Al Woodall (back to camera) and coaches Wimp Hewgley and Ken Meyer

leadership

In order to be a leader, the first thing you have to have is confidence in what you're doing. You have to know your job, have complete knowledge of your offense and what you can do with it in any situation. You can't step into the huddle and start to sputter—stutter around and change your mind and just grope. To be a leader you have to make people want to follow you, and nobody wants to follow somebody who doesn't know where he's going.

So every time you step in that huddle, you've got to know what to call. The way to do that is to study up until you know your offense and their defense, and the right call comes to you just naturally.

What's the difference between being confident and egotistical?

There's a fine line between confidence and cockiness. I'm a confident guy. If I go out there and throw ten incomplete passes in a row, I'm coming right back and throw the eleventh. That's right. I know what I can do.

But that doesn't mean I'm cocky. Pro football can be a tough game on a cocky guy because no matter how good you are, everybody gets put down from time to time. It's part of the game. So you have to display a confidence and a knowledge about the game and go about things with a direct attitude—

what you are doing is right and you know it is right. But you don't have the attitude that the play is going to work because *you* are going to make it work. That's cockiness. You don't mean, "I'll make it work." You mean, "*We'll* make it work." You know you're calling the right play because of the whole team you've got against the whole team they've got. And if that's your attitude, your teammates are going to believe you and go about their jobs with an all-out effort.

What happens if you don't have the confidence?

That can be a bad feeling. It happened to me one time that I think of in particular, and I'm not going to say whether this was pro or college or whatever, but it was a long time ago. We were down pretty good at halftime and the team that was beating us was a solid football team. That's a tough situation, behind two or three touchdowns to a good team. How are you going to catch up? It's depressing.

You come out on the field for the second half and the guys are saying, "Come on. Let's go. We can get them," and you say, "Yeah, yeah, right, let's go." But the drive isn't there. And the half goes by and you find yourself catching up until finally at the end you have a chance of winning. That's what happened to us. We got close, and then we didn't win. We just missed.

And that's a bad feeling. In a situation like that, you're by yourself. It's your fault. If I'd have had the confidence, if I'd have believed in myself and the team and gone out there fighting for my life, we might have won.

We almost won as it was. And you say to yourself, "You jerk, you blew that game." And one lesson like that should be enough. A quarterback has to have confidence in himself and his teammates all the time, no matter what the situation. That's the only way he can lead them when things get tight.

What can you do if the team is not performing well?

What you have to do when things are getting screwed up is tell the guys what is happening. You are the quarterback and you know the game better than they do. A guard might know his job better than you know his job, but you know the overall scope better than anybody. If things aren't going right, you should be the first one to understand it. Then you have to convey it to the team in a way they can understand it—and do something about it.

You can't handle the situation in a way that just screws things up worse, that adds to the confusion or comes on like panic. You have to do it in a way that is simple and direct and strong, and get those guys to know what they have to do.

When things start to go bad, if we get beat a few plays consistently and we're making mental errors and things like that, I get ticked off. I get mighty upset when that happens. And I just have to get it across to the team what's going on and

A quarterback has confidence in his teammates as well as in his own ability

that it's got to stop and that we have to get rolling.

Does it do much good to get mad?

I don't say get mad. Dogs get mad. People get angry. I can get real angry but I still keep my head together. You're out there working and you have ten other guys to work with.

But there's not much time, either. It doesn't take them much time to show me they are screwing up. If some guy misses a block, I know about it right quick. And it doesn't take me long to let those guys know what's happening either. I tell them, "What the hell! What are you suckers doing? Let's get working out here!"

You can't fake it. You can't holler at people just to be hollering. If you really get upset at something, you can let them know. But you don't just go screaming at people as a general practice and you'd better not humiliate them, tell some guy he's a punk or a coward. These guys are some of the best football players in the country and they've been playing all their lives. They know what their job is and by and large there's not much a quarterback has to do to get them to play. But now and then, at some point in the game, you might sense a low ebb, sense when things aren't functioning and jelling. You can feel it happening and it ticks you off and you have to let everybody know just how it is.

How do you handle different individuals?

Everybody on a team is different. They're all human beings and they all react differently in different situations and a quarterback has to know how to deal with each guy to get the best out of him.

Some guys, it doesn't do any good to holler at them at all. They have a certain kind of pride where if they get beat, they automatically want to gear up for the next play. All you have to do is check with them to see what happened, see if they know that they screwed up. But you don't have to get on them. They'll take care of themselves.

Other guys are different. Maybe they can get inspired by another guy yelling at them. They hear a lot of stuff out of the quarterback and that fires them up and they say, "All right, this play I'm really going to kill my man." Or there's some guys who can lose their concentration, start making mental errors. Sometimes you can shake those guys out of it. "You want to play out here? Start thinking or get yourself the hell of the field."

Every guy is different and every situation is different and all you can do is try to react to what is actually going on. It's like if you open your front door in the morning and some neighborhood kid is there and he's broken a bottle of milk on your porch. Maybe he kicked it accidentally and it fell over, or maybe he just picked it up and dropped it on purpose. Whatever happened, you have to react accordingly. It's the same with a quarterback. You can't just decide to be a tough guy and start screaming at people no matter what. But you can't stand around and let things slide when guys are screwing up, either. You have to get a sense for what's happening and then come on with how you really feel.

How do you know when to step in as leader?

A quarterback has to have a feel for the game. You have to sense the game, pick up on the pace of it, find where the momentum is and learn how to handle it. It's like in a rock band the drummer has to take care of the beat—get things rolling when they're slow or back things off if they get too frantic. A quarterback has to feel the flow of the game and move things around to keep the pace going right for whatever the situation is.

Every game's different. Every game's a new adventure. You have to find out what type of game it is, how the guys are reacting to the situation, and make things go accordingly. If you've got the game under control, you have to keep things cool and moving efficiently. If you're dragging a little, you might have to speed things up, get some spark happening. How you act depends on what you feel.

How do you react when things are moving well?

If the team is hitting good, if the holes are opening and the passes are working, I feel brisk. It's a good feeling. We're rolling. At a time like that I work to keep the momentum up. Get in and out of the huddle in a hurry, keep the pace moving. Maybe we'll even call a few "Check-with-me" plays so we don't stay in the huddle more than a few seconds. I'll just call the plays at the line. We've got the defense on the run and they're back in their huddle calling a defense and here we are coming out at them already. Maybe we can get them upset by coming at them and coming at them, staying on top of them.

At a time like that I try to stay with plays I know are working, stay with the straight stuff, keep on rolling. I eliminate reverses and even sweeps and screens sometimes, any kind of play that might lose some yardage.

On passes maybe I might emphasize quick hitting passes, outs and slants and things like that, but I've got a lot of confidence in our passing in general. I'd call most any pass I thought would work. If my main man isn't open I've always got a few more guys I can find and even if I don't find anybody I can always try to throw the ball away and keep from losing yards. I'm definitely not wanting to get sacked in a situation like that. The ball is going to get thrown somewhere, whether to one of my people or to some open field, because I don't want to lose ten yards when we've got things happening. I don't ever want to get sacked, but a time like that it's just terrible.

A quarterback must make things clear

Guard Dave Herman is one of the many different personalities on the team and the quarterback has to be able to relate to them all constructively

How do you react if things aren't going well?

If things aren't happening out there, you just have to get it going. If we've been stopped a couple of times, I try to find out what's the matter and so do the coaches. Maybe it's the game plan. Maybe the defense is doing some things we didn't expect and they're screwing us up. Hopefully we're capable enough to adjust out there while the game's going on. That's why our game plans are pretty general. We have a lot of stuff we can use, even if we were planning to use a few things specifically, and we just have to look at what they're doing and react with the kind of plays that will go against them.

Or maybe the plan's all right, but you are just getting yourselves beat man for man. If that's what's happening—they're just putting it on you—well, damn, you've got to talk to one another and get your butt in gear and work like hell. The quarterback's got to do some talking, get some adrenalin flowing. Tell them where we're screwing up and what we have to do and just lay it out to them.

When you get that cleared up, then you just try to run plays where you're going to be going one-on-one. At least that's what I do. Straight man-to-man blocking where it's all up to individual effort. Challenge each guy with the assignment. Don't call any plays where guys have to pull or criss-cross or something where they might slip or trip on some-

Flanker Don Maynard

count around to throw them off and you've got to get them off you with some passes, open them up. If you see where you have a chance at a long one, go ahead and throw it. Even if you miss you might back them up a little and get your short passing game happening and then start to get some running after that.

The one thing you want to avoid at a time like this, when things aren't moving right, is giving up the ball. A turnover's bad any time but it's really bad then. It's one thing to lose momentum and be stymied for awhile, but to get bottled up at your own end and not get anything going and then drop the ball or throw it to the other team, that really does kill you. It's like the field is tipped up and running downhill toward your goal line.

Tight end Richard Caster

body's foot or have some kind of excuse like that. Just put the hat on each guy and make him go and want to perform. "We're going to blow right at them now, damn it. Let's get something established. It's just us and them."

If that doesn't work, you have to keep trying. Go to the old passing game. Maybe the defense is up close on you and feeling confident and coming hard. You can keep changing your

Halfback Emerson Boozer

What makes a quarterback good at handling the pace of the game?

This is something a quarterback can work on, think about ahead of time like anything else. If you've thought things through ahead of time, it's easier to handle situations when they come up on the field.

But this is also something that comes with experience, just being in situations before and when they come up again you know better how to react. And it depends on who the quarterback is. Some of these things come naturally, feeling what's happening and knowing how to react. It's a question of a guy's personality as much as anything. There's no one way to handle the problem. Each guy has to react in ways that are natural to him and his way of doing things.

calling the plays

Talking about calling signals, I'd like to emphasize one thing. The overall game situation pretty much dictates to a quarterback what he should do. A good quarterback is a quarterback who reacts correctly to the situation when it confronts him.

There's a lot of strategy and thinking to football, but it's not like chess or mathematics, where things are more cut and dried. When I'm calling plays, I can't just decide what I think is the best play right now in a theoretical way. All sorts of things have to come into my thinking. Who's ahead? What's the field position? What down is it? How many yards? What's the time? What's the weather like? Who's injured? Who's tired?

Each new down is a new situation. Some factors may stay the same, like which team is ahead, but other factors change, like yards to go or who is injured. I have to keep in mind the whole situation and react to that situation in the best way I can.

What about other approaches to play calling?

I realize everybody doesn't agree with this way of looking at it. Some people like to call plays in a pre-planned sequence they use one after another in a series. Maybe they run off tackle, then they fake a run off tackle and go around end, then they fake an end run and pass. The idea is to get some plays together that set each other up, so you can use one or two to get a team off balance and then hit them with your stinger.

It's not that I wouldn't like to do this. But it's just damn hard to make a series of plays work any more. Defenses jump around so much, giving you different looks every time, that it's hard to get anything like a series established. They show you one defense and you run a play and then you call the counter off that play and come out to the line and they are in some other defense altogether and your counter play isn't worth a damn.

Over the course of a game, maybe, you can set something up. Maybe you notice that twice when they have been in a certain defense, you have run an end run. Then fifteen minutes later you come up to the line and there they are in that defense again, so you audible to a fake end run thinking they will expect it, and then run up the center. It might work. Sometimes you can use a sequence of plays like that, all out of sequence. You have to retain what has happened earlier in the game.

But as for coming out with some definite set of plays you have in mind and just running them one after another, usually you can't do it. Every down is a new situation. Suppose on first down you try to sweep and the guy loses five yards and now it's second and 15. Are you going to come back with your planned off-tackle play? I probably wouldn't unless there was some special reason. Second and 15 I've got to get some yards.

That's why I call plays to fit the situation, not a sequence. If I come up to second and 15, I have a group of plays already in my head that we want to run against this team in a long-yardage situation on second down. I pick one of those and go with it. The next time it's second and long, I go back to the same group of plays again and choose the one that makes the most sense. Maybe one of the plays in the group is a screen to the right and I've noticed that their linebacker on that side is limping a little. Well, that's part of the situation, too, so that may be the direction of my attack.

A quarterback can't force his ideas onto the game. He has to see the situation and react to it. **When did calling plays to situations first seem important?**

There was one game in my career where I really learned to pay attention to the whole situation in a way that I hadn't up to that time. This was in our Super Bowl season in 1968. We had started off winning our first two games and we went up to Buffalo to play the Bills. Now with the team we had at that time and the team they had at that time, we figured to win. Sure enough we came out throwing and got ahead and we kept on throwing and piled up 35 points. But the thing was I also threw five interceptions and several of them set up scores for Buffalo and we wound up losing the game 37-35.

That was a terrible feeling and after the game our defensive coach came up to me and said, "Joe, you didn't have to throw the ball so much. You didn't have to take chances like that because they couldn't move the ball very well on our defense. We knew before the game they couldn't score much on us."

I was really down. "Hell," I said. "I wish you'd told me that before the game. I wasn't even thinking about that, about how our defense was going to do. I was only thinking about how we could score points."

But I learned a lesson right there. What the other team's offense can do against *your* defense is just as important as what you can do against *their* defense. It's all part of the situation, the total picture. And you have to keep it in mind when you call plays. Why take chances trying to hit a big play if you are pretty sure the other team isn't going to score much anyway?

How do you call plays if the game is in hand?

I played the rest of that year thinking about our defense, too, not just our offense. I still do. Even though our defense hasn't always been as good as it was in 1968 and 1969, there have been games where we got in control and our running game was going good and I just stuck with it. I only threw 12 times in one game

A quarterback has to keep the whole situation in mind—not just what the scoreboard shows but also any information from the coaches overhead

against New England, I remember. We didn't have to pass much so why try? I called running plays and ran the clock.

Sometimes it's a little hard to make yourself do this, to stick on the ground, even if the situation calls for it. You get a little restless, you feel like trying something you see. You've been running, running, running, and now it seems like time to throw. But why? Why take the chance?

What happens if the other team comes back?

It's possible to get in trouble now and then when you play conservatively and try to run the clock. Things can seem pretty smooth and then suddenly the other team does a couple of things and gets back in the game. It hasn't happened to me much but it can happen. In fact, it did happen that same year in 1968 after we had blown to Buffalo. But I always have confidence we can score if we have to. If the other team makes it tough, we can open up and do what we need.

In that game I'm talking about, we were on top of Houston 13-0 the whole second half. This was three weeks after the Buffalo game and we just stayed pretty basic with our calls and tried to get to the final gun — a strategy that made pretty good sense because I didn't hit anything the first ten passes I threw. But then in the fourth quarter they took out their quarterback and put in Bob Davis, who's with us now in New York. Davis came in and threw some good passes and scrambled all over everywhere

and suddenly Houston had 14 points. We were behind 14-13 and there was only a minute thirty-five to go.

That's the only time that happened to me, where a team came back like that and actually took the lead, but it worked out all right because we took the ball and drove it 80 yards and scored a touchdown. It was tight but we got out of it. I remember the lady standing outside the dressing room that time. This was in Houston and she was an Oiler fan and she said, "Oh, Joe, I thought you were going to let us win." She was really put down, but she finally said, "Oh, well, good game anyway." I appreciated that.

What about times when you can't play safe?

You can't always try to be safe with a lead, of course. Against some teams — Dallas, San Diego, Oakland, teams like that — you know they can explode any time. They can put up two or three touchdowns in a hurry and so even if you are ahead you have to keep working for openings, take your chances to get some more points.

And then, unfortunately, you're not always ahead. If you get behind or if your running game isn't going well, you have to start throwing and keep throwing. The whole situation can be reversed completely. Like that Monday night Oakland game in 1972. All our runners were hurt one way or the other and what was I going to do but throw the ball? What's the use of calling a running play to keep them honest if we can't run anyway and it isn't going to keep

them honest? You've just got to to out and throw and throw.

That's hard business. It's pretty tough to pass if they know you can't run and they can just flood back into your passing lanes and turn their defensive line loose to rush the passer. I threw 40 something times in that game against Oakland but hell, I've thrown as much as 62 times on one day. That was against the Colts in 1970 when Johnny Unitas got them 17 points ahead right away and we had our runners hurt and there wasn't anything else to do. They held on then 29-22 with the help of some more interceptions.

Or there was the game when Unitas was playing so well and they scored 34 points. The last two times we got the ball I threw the bomb on first down and we hit both of them to win 44-34. We were ahead three points each time but I wasn't going to sit on any lead with Unitas doing his thing. Johnny's beautiful the way he can work a team, keep you off balance and move the ball. Any time you play him, he's part of the situation. You have to keep him in mind all the time.

How can the snap count help your plays work?

A quarterback should use his snap count as an offensive weapon. The count is not just a way of making sure the whole offense gets off together. It can also be used to help set up certain plays, or to keep the defense off balance and give your guys a jump.

Your own defense affects your play calling and Al Atkinson and Gerry Philbin have helped the Jet defense for a number of years

I have to be careful about it. It's possible to get into habits where you always call the same plays on the same count. You have to keep thinking about it. You can't let those defensive guys get a line on you and just start blowing in full bore.

It's especially important to vary the count in passing situations where they want to just tee off and get to you. You have to mix it up, get off on a quick count one time, then hold on for a long one the next time.

How can the quick count be a problem?

If I want the team to go on a quick count, I won't have a chance to audible when I get up to the line; the play will start before I get to the part of our count where we call the audibles. Our usual signals go like this: "Shift (backs shift); Red 38 Red 38 (an audible or fake audible); Four Three (the defensive line-up); Ready (team goes down in stance); Hut, Hut, Hut, etc." In the huddle, I can tell them we'll start the play on any of those parts of the count. And if I say we'll go on "Shift"—a quick count—I'm never going to get to the audible part. That means I'm locked in with the play I have called.

And that's why, when I'm going on a quick count, I usually call a basic play, probably a straight-blocking run play, or a basic pass play that's going to be pretty good no matter what defense they run. If I call some fancy play, a counter or a sucker play, whatever, and they show me a defense that is just going to kill the play, I haven't got any way to get out of it. I try not to box myself into that situation.

A quarterback has to work his snap count to give his offense an edge

How can the count help on a draw or screen?

Usually when we run a draw play or screen pass, a play that begins as a fake pass, we want to make sure the defense is coming in full speed. So we try to run those on a normal count— like two (the second Hut). That's a count the defense is used to having us use and they can get a pretty good jump blowing in after me. That's just what we want, of course, so they'll over- run the draw or screen. This is Weeb Ewbank's idea and it makes sense to me. The only time we'd go away from this is maybe if we've run a few passes on the quick count and the defense has got used to that by the time we call the draw or screen.

What about clutch situations?

Any time it's a crucial third down in a short yardage situa- tion, or say when we're down inside their ten and working for a touchdown, that's a time we really don't want to blow a count. A guy jumps there and five yards can seem like fifty. So when we're in situations like that, I'll usually go on a count that the team is used to so I don't screw them up. I don't want them worrying about the snap. I want them worrying about doing their jobs. Or if I do want to use a long count, maybe, to try to draw the other team offside, then I'll really overemphasize it in the huddle, say it two or three times.

How can field position affect your play calling?

Where you are on the field is obviously very important in play selection. You have to keep your position in mind all the time. It's part of the situation. However, I think some teams may play field position a little more cautiously than we do. Even if I'm right back on my own goal-line, I'll pass if I think I can hit it. I have a lot of confidence in our passing attack and I'll go to it any time anywhere if I see something good.

But I do keep field position in mind. When I was at Alabama, Paul Bryant had a theory about different field position "zones" that makes sense to me, and I'll pass it along here.

Using Bryant's system, the first area on the field is the "Get Out" zone. That's a little one starting on your own goal line and going out to the three-yard line. Down there that close, boy, you've just got to get out at least a few yards so if you have to punt, your punter can stand his normal depth.

When things are that tight, you have to be careful what kind of runs you use. Sweeps and quick pitches can lose yardage and get you a safety down there. Certain kinds of trap plays, too—where one of your linemen pulls out to block—can let a linebacker blitz through the hole the lineman leaves and nail your runner for a loss. You usually stick to runs where you're almost guaranteed of getting to the line of scrimmage.

The next area of the field goes from the three to the twenty. This is the Danger Zone. Even though there's not quite the chance of getting hit for a safety, still a fumble or an interception down here is almost a sure score for the other team. So you have to keep alert and don't use any fancy plays where there is a bigger chance of error.

From your own twenty-yard line to the other team's twenty, the whole big center of the field, Bryant calls that the Free Wheeling Zone. That's the area where you can cut loose, pull out anything you've got and give it a try. You don't want to louse up here any more than you do anywhere else, but the consequences of a mistake aren't so disastrous in the middle of the field and so you want to take the opportunity to put the heat on the other team, go after them with your best stuff and make them stop it.

From the opposition twenty on in to the goal line, that's the Gut Zone. This is where you've earned yourself a scoring chance and you have to gut that ball in there some way. It's also an area where you want to avoid the mental error or the big penalty that are going to cost you downs and yards and wreck your scoring chance. It's up to the quarterback to make sure that everybody concentrates in the Gut Zone.

The situation in pro ball, of course, is not the same as it is in high school and college. Although I think Bryant's zone system is good, if I see something good and the overall situation is right, I'm going to call it no matter what my field position because I'm running a pro team and I know we have the capability to execute.

In the pros, I also have to keep the field goal situation in my head all the time. Often in college you don't have a good kicker, but most every pro team does, and I have to try to help him, too. On the other team's thirty, for instance, I might not call a reverse. A reverse could lose ten yards and get us out of good field goal range. I also emphasize not getting sacked in that position for the same reason.

Is it easier to score from the five or the thirty-five?

It might seem logical that every yard you get closer to the end zone makes it that much easier to get the ball in. But this isn't always true. I'm not going to refuse any first downs on the five-yard line, but if you stop to think about it you've got a problem trying to move from that close in. Counting the ten yards of end zone, you only have fifteen yards of field to work with. The defensive guys can come up faster on runs and short passes because they know you can't get deep behind them. In some ways, that means it's easier to score from farther out. You have more room to work with and they have more to cover.

This doesn't mean that as soon as I get down to the twenty or thirty I'm going to throw three downs in a row and take my chances. I might go on

grinding it out, provided this is good for us at that point or our defense is holding them well. But if I feel we need to get the quick points or if I think their defense will get a lot tougher closer in, I'll be more likely to try to get it all in one play.

How can field conditions affect play calling?

Unfortunately, football is not like pool. Anytime you've got a good pool table, you know the balls are going to roll true and if you hit the ball right you're going to get something in the pocket. But playing football you have to deal with a bunch of factors that don't have much to do with the physical and mental talent of your team. You expect a nice day, but you get outside and the temperature is 20 degrees and it's snowing and the field is a mess and the wind is blowing a ton and how are you supposed to play a game in conditions like that? The way things are these days, you can go out on a perfect day and play on one of these plastic fields and slip all over like it was a mud bowl.

There aren't any good answers to problems like this. You just go out and play, do the best you can, and try to disregard some of the aspects of the weather. Now I said disregard some of the weather. You shouldn't disregard the footing or the wind conditions.

How do you handle bad footing?

One thing we do is go all over the field before the game and draw the field up on the chalk board in the locker room and mark in any areas that are

There's nothing to do in the rain but keep trying to throw the ball normally

sloppy. When you're playing in areas like that, you have to cut down on complicated stuff. You don't want to run plays where your linemen have to pull out sideways or where your backs are crossing, things like that. You tend to go with basic straight-ahead stuff until you get out of the muck. Or you might sweep out of the area if things are better over on the other side of the field.

The wind, of course, can be a factor anywhere on the field. It can be a drag trying to pass in a heavy wind, and we get that kind a lot of the time in Shea Stadium. When it's blowing pretty good, you have to change your play-calling depending on whether it's coming at your face or at your back.

When I have a following wind, I tend to speed up the tempo and get off as many plays as I can. That kind of wind isn't nearly so hard on my passing as a wind in my face—unless I float a long ball—so I go ahead and call my full game and do it quickly. The point is that if I'm stopped, I still want my punter to have the wind to kick with. If the wind is against me, on the other hand, I slow things up and run the ball a lot and try to get out of the quarter so my kicker won't have so much trouble.

Is running or passing more advantageous?

When I first came up I got a reputation as a guy who likes to throw all the time. There was something to that because we didn't have all that good a team then and we had to throw a lot. The year before we went to the Super Bowl, we ran up over 4,000 yards passing.

But the fact is, I don't especially like to pass if I don't have to. If the game is tough and I have to pass all the time that's not a good feeling. I can't ever get comfortable out there. Like that Monday night in Oakland I had to throw over and over and every situation was critical and there wasn't any time to relax and run a comfortable game. I don't necessarily like that, having all that tension all the time.

I don't like to pass especially— I like to win.

It's a challenge to throw the ball, to try to solve a defense and find a receiver and put the ball to him. It's hard to do and it's a good feeling to do it well. But it's also a good feeling to just run a team right, call the right plays, keep the tempo working smooth.

I don't mind throwing if it's time to throw and I don't mind running if it's time to run. I've gone a whole half without ever throwing once and I've thrown 62 times in one game. The only thing is to win the game. I don't get paid for records or statistics. I've never been in that bag. I just do what the situation calls for and try to win the game—an attitude I got from good training, a good coaching background.

audibles

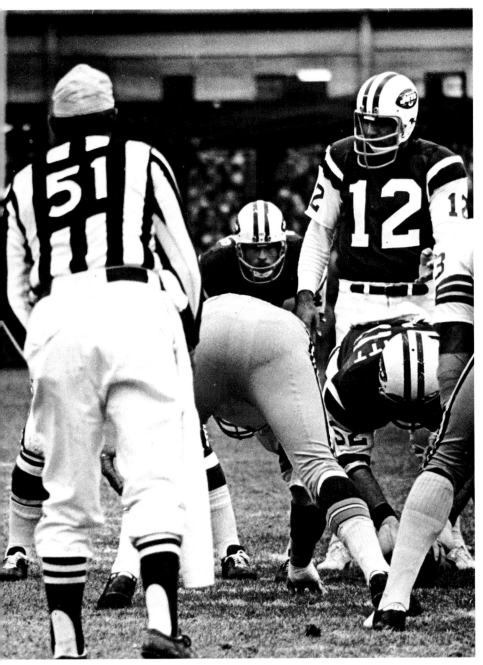

Up at the line a quarterback has to check the whole defense over to see, for instance, how to handle a defensive tackle who is lined up tight

By the word "audible" I mean a situation where I get up to the line of scrimmage, get the team set, and then call out a number that tells the team what play we are going to run. Everybody can hear the play, including the defense, which is why it's called an audible. Naturally, we need to use some sort of code so the defense can't catch on to what we're doing, but I'll get into that later.

Why use audibles?

The reason I like to use audibles is that I can put off my final decision on what play to use until the last possible second. Usually I have a play called in the huddle, then I go up to the line and look those guys over on defense and see if what I've called looks good or not. I change the play right then if I see something better.

Defenses throw a lot of stuff at you these days. The linemen shift one way or the other, some of them are up close to the line and some of them lay off a yard back. Linebackers move all over the place and the secondaries slip into every kind of pass coverage they can think of. Of course, we can beat every defense there is. There's always something we can do, there's always a weakness in every defense. Our problem is that we're never sure in advance which defense the other team is going to use on a given play. We have an idea. We know what they *like* to use in given situations. But we can't ever be sure.

That's why I audible. I can get up there behind center and take a look for myself. Where are these guys? What are they doing? Where are they leaving me a hole? Even at the line, of course, I can't always tell everything about a defense. They could still stunt their linemen after the play starts and they can sometimes hide what pass coverage they are going to run. But the view from up there is sure better than the one back in the huddle.

What is the key factor in calling audibles?

The most important thing I need as a quarterback to make the audible system work is the confidence to call what I see. There it is, boy, jump on it right now. Don't wait. Don't hesitate. If I see it, call it. What I'm saying now depends on the situation to some extent. I mean I wouldn't necessarily be completely aggressive if I already had a game under control and I just wanted to stick to sound, basic stuff.

But if we're still scrambling and I see something good, I'll call it. Say I go up to the line and I've got a run called in the huddle and it looks pretty good versus the defense they're in. But say I also see where they are lined up to use a certain pass coverage that is going to leave my left end covered man-to-man. Even if my running play looks good, if I can see what pass coverage they are using, nuts to the run. I'll check to a pass play. I'll jump on that man-to-man, call a quick post, or a post-corner or something to go after that defensive guy. Hell, we don't

see enough man-to-man any more where we can afford to let it go by if we know it's coming.

How do you keep the defense from picking up your audibles?

There are several different systems, but we use a color system in New York. I come out to the line and holler a color and a number, like Blue 37, Blue 37. I call it out twice, once left and once right. If blue is a "live" color that week, then we will run the 37 play. If blue is not a "live" color that week, we go ahead and run whatever play I had called in the huddle. We just ignore the 37.

Each week we have three live colors. We might have Red, Orange and Yellow; or Black, White and Grey; or Red, White and Blue. We try to pick some colors that seem to go together so they are easy to remember. Having three colors like that makes it just about impossible for the defense to find out which colors are actually going to be live.

I do check up on it to make sure they're not picking up on what we're doing. If a linebacker gets into a hole faster than I expect, or a lineman chases a run super fast, I might think about whether our audibles are being picked up. We've changed colors at halftime before, maybe once or twice. But it hardly ever happens, and if it does I can just run a few "Check-with-me" plays to confuse them.

What is a "Check-with-me"?

Sometimes during a game, maybe twenty per cent of the time, I'll get in the huddle, give a formation and then just say, "Check with me." That means we're going out to the line in a formation but with no play, and

I'm going to call the play right at the line. In a situation like that, it doesn't matter what color I call. We don't have a play yet, so anything is live. I could call, "Heliotrope," and whatever number I called, that's the play we'd run. If the defense is guessing with us, this will screw them up because for that play any color is live. They can't get a line on us.

Running a "Check-with-me" play has another advantage, too. It makes me think up at the line. If my head has been getting a little slow and I haven't been jumping on the defense, going after the weaknesses, a "Check-with-me" will gear me up. I *have* to call a play at the line, so I *have* to find a weakness. It keeps me alert. We aren't ever running a play that is bad against the defense. Actually, we could run most of our offense from the line and sometimes I'll do it for awhile, call "Check-with-me" a few times, just to speed up the tempo.

How can you have a number for all the different plays you have?

It's really pretty simple. We have our running plays in series —the 20 series, the 30 series, etc. A 28 play requires 20 series action by the backs—maybe the fullback going to the weak side of the quarterback and the halfback going to the strong side— with the play going into the 8 hole, out wide around right end. It's a standard kind of play-numbering system. If there is a variation on the play, like the tackle pulling instead of the guard, for instance, I can take care of that with one letter. I'd call out 28 T instead of just 28.

On passes, the same thing. We have the 70 pass, the 71 pass, the 72 pass, and so forth, each one with different receivers going out into different areas. If I want one or two receivers to change off the basic pass, I just call out letters after the number. It's nothing new for anybody to learn because even in the huddle we call our patterns by letter. I'll say "Flanker Q," instead of "Flanker square out 15." All our receivers know the letters so at the line I can just call out "72Q" one way and maybe "72L" the other way and I have the basic 72 pattern, with two guys doing individual routes off it. There's nothing hard about the system, as long as I can see what I want to do.

How can you use fake audibles?

You can sometimes confuse a defense with fake audibles. On that 28 play for instance, it's pretty standard around the league that 28 would be some kind of play out around end. So in the huddle maybe I'll call a fake end run with a handoff inside of tackle. Then I'll go out to the line and use some dead color like brown and yell, "Brown 28, Brown 28," using a number that sounds like an end run. When the play starts to look like an end run, we might just get some guy leaning a little more than usual and then hit back up inside of him. You don't really know, but it's worth a shot. If they start listening to your audibles, you can mess their heads around pretty well.

I remember one time a couple of years ago when it worked

perfectly. We were playing a team with a coach who used to coach our offensive line, and we thought the coach had probably told them our audible system. We got down on about the five and it was third down and I called a run right up the middle, expecting them to be in a defense they like to use down there with nobody lined up right over center. Well, we came out and everybody on their team looked like they were in that defense except the middle guard. He was standing right in the middle. I figured he was probably faking me, that he was going to jump over to the right where he was supposed to be just as the play started, but just to be sure I called out a fake audible, audible 57. At that time 57 for us was a pickoff pass over on our right, with the flanker angling in. I figured the linebacker probably had been told about it because we liked to use it on the goal line. I even went, "57P," P for pickoff, just to make it sure. And you ought to see it in the films. The play starts and that middle linebacker just jets out to the right. Nobody touched our runner going up the middle. I don't think the linebacker ever saw the guy go. Whoosh, five yards on third down, touchdown.

That's the kind of thing you can get into with fake audibles after a while. It takes time. You need experience up there. You need to know your own offense down pat, you need to know what the defense is doing and why. And your mind has to be just racing full speed. But the more you practice it during the week, calling fakes that seem to

help you, like calling out a 70 or 80 series fake audible complete with letters, like it's a pass, and then going ahead with the draw play you have called, the more you do that, the more it comes to you. It's a question of getting your head together. You have to work on it.

Can high school teams and quarterbacks use an audible system?

Audibles can work in high school. There's just a couple of things you have to make sure of. First off, the plays should be called the same way in the huddle and at the line, so nobody has to learn anything new.

Second, the quarterback has to have complete command of his offense, know all the plays so that if he sees a weakness he can call the play right now. If the quarterback doesn't have all the plays right at his fingertips, he can't run the audible system well at all.

Third, he has to know why to run certain plays against certain defenses. This is where the coach comes in. A lot of times coaches just tell their boys, "Run this," without telling them why. If you don't tell a quarterback why you want something, it doesn't help him enough. But if you tell him why, then he has a handle on it, he can remember. Like you tell him to run a trap. Why? Because that one defensive lineman is charging hard and we can hit him from the side and make yards. Or you tell him to throw slant-in passes against a three-deep pass

defense. Why? Because there is no safetyman in there to help out with the inside seam. If the quarterback knows why, the idea makes sense and he can retain it better.

A final thing to remember if you use audibles part of the time is to be sure to call some of your basic plays—where you won't need to audible—on the quick count. You want to do this so the defense can't get in the habit of jumping around during your count and messing up your audibles. If you go on the quick count some of the time, they won't have time to jump around.

If a quarterback has command of his plays and knows why to call each one against certain defenses, there's no reason he can't run an audible system. All he has to do is practice it instead of calling all the plays in the huddle. Run a lot of "Check-with-me" plays in practice to get used to it. If he's already played one year and knows the system, it ought to be easy. The rest of the team doesn't have to learn anything new at all. But they do have to be alert.

The principle is the same for a high school quarterback as it is for me. He has to decide what play to call and it's easier for him after he's seen what the other team is doing, the same as it is for me. Good play calling is reacting to the situation with the right play, and it's easier to get up to the line and really see the situation than to sit back in the huddle and try to imagine what it will be.

I usually get down over center quickly, but if the receivers have trouble hearing audibles I will stand up to shout them out clearly

163

the running game

I'm not the type who thinks you have to go out every game and start grinding away with your running attack to show the other team you can do it. If you've got a running game, the other team knows it before the game starts anyway. But you have to be able to run and over a whole season you must balance up your attack.

How do you call the running game?

I've never had much trouble calling the running game. It's a straightforward procedure. You have to get to know the defenses and the personnel of the other team, learn which plays you have that are good against those various defenses and people, and in what situation, and then call the play accordingly.

In the huddle you usually have a pretty good idea of which of their defenses they are likely to use because you have studied up on their habits as a team. Maybe on first down they tend to run an overshift to the strong side. You call one of your plays for that defense, like a slant back to the weak side, and then go out to the line of scrimmage. If you get up there and they are in some other defense, you just check off to one of your plays that is good against that setup. I practice doing this all week six months a year and there would have to be something wrong with me if I couldn't do it reasonably well.

In a whole game I'll only do one thing that is something more than just this sort of reaction. Now and then I'll deliberately call a play that doesn't look too good against the defense they've chosen. I do that on purpose to screw up their thinking, so they

A good running attack helps the passing, and John Riggins helps a lot

can't figure out the pattern of my play calling. Remember, the other team scouts us as much as we scout them, and if I always called the same few plays against the same defenses, the defense could "key" on me and figure out in advance what I was going to do. Throwing in something a little weird as a "key breaker" gives them something to think about.

Do you run at defenses or personnel?

When I'm calling plays I have to keep both the defensive alignment and the defensive players in mind all the time. If a defense has overshifted one way, for instance, it usually makes sense to run the other way. If a defense is in a balanced 4-3 alignment, it might be easier to use certain kinds of traps. But in either case, you can't look at those defenses like they are X's and O's on the chalk board. There are people in those defensive spots and people have characteristics, and you should know how to take advantage of their characteristics.

Maybe the defense overshifts, but maybe the middle guy in the overshift isn't physically as strong as the blocker you have there. Well, hell, you go with your personnel advantage and run at the overshift.

You must know their personnel. Which of their linemen charge hard across the line where you can hit them from the side with a trap block? Which of their linebackers is weaker or stronger at taking on a blocker one-on-one and still being able to make the play. How conscious are their ends of stopping the sweep? Can you power inside them?

There are a lot of questions like this, and you have to have them all answered and memorized long before you get out there where the action is.

Besides running through all the plays in practice, I also give myself a series of tests each week. When I've got time on the bus going to practice, or sitting around in my kitchen waiting for an evening to start, I'll write down every defense the team is going to use against me and under every defense I write down all the plays we want to use against that defense. I do it over and over until it all just comes by second nature. By the time I see their defense on Sunday, I've already been there. I react to what I see right now.

Should you run plays at a defense's strength?

I've read where Vince Lombardi used to think you should run at the strength of a defense because if you could break down the strongest part, the whole thing would fold up. That makes some sense, I suppose, but we don't usually do it. We've been pretty successful running at a team where we think we can beat them—either beat their alignment or else beat some of their personnel.

I know on passes you don't ever want to go at the strength of a defense because what you mean by strength in pass defense is the place where the defense

has the most people. You never want to throw into a crowd.

In the running game, however, you go at strength now and then to keep them honest. If they are overshifted one way, now and then you go ahead and run at the overshift to keep them from just slanting down like crazy back to their weak side after the play starts. Or if they have a great lineman, you should run at him now and then to keep him entertained so he doesn't start wandering around and tearing you up all over the place.

Should a running game be complex or simple?

Some teams, like the Dallas Cowboys or the Kansas City Chiefs, often run a complicated rushing attack, with a lot of false blocking and influence blocking and counter plays and reverses. They make it work well, and so

Emerson Boozer is still one of the most effective cutback runners

do some other teams. On the Jets, however, our running game is pretty basic. A lot of our plays are just straight ahead man-on-man blocking and our runners just go up in there and go where they can find the most room. We do some other things, but basic running is the guts of our attack. It depends on strong blockers and the kind of runner who can adjust to what he sees.

This kind of attack makes the play calling reasonably orderly. We just go after them at the place where we feel we have an advantage either in personnel or formation. And if we get something going, we'll stay with it a lot until they do something to stop it. You may remember the Super Bowl game in 1969 when Matt Snell got rolling on a slant to our left behind Emerson Boozer and tackle Winston Hill. Boozer and Hill are great blockers and Snell ran the play well and we were just beating them over there the way they were playing us.

It seems to me that when you get something rolling like that, you might as well stick with it. Maybe not play after play, but then again maybe you'll call the same thing two or three plays in a row.

Sometimes it gets tough to control yourself in a situation like this. There's a temptation to try something new that you think might be good, or something you used before that was nearly successful. But if you've got a good thing going, it's the quarterback's job to work it, to get the most out of it. If the defense can't stop the play, why should *you* stop it?

the passing game

Whatever happened to single coverage? I asked that earlier in this book but it didn't seem to help any. Whatever happened to the days when you could isolate one receiver on one defensive back, run three fakes on the guy and beat him for the big play touchdown? I don't see much of it any more, I'll tell you that. You have to work harder to get your scores now than ever.

Actually, I think I do know what happened to single coverage. We beat the hell out of it. There were several good passing teams there in the late Sixties, and we were one of them, and the success we had throwing to our wide receivers is a big part of the reason why the defenses decided to double up on wide receivers and try to take them out of the offense.

On the Jets, we had Don Maynard on one side and George Sauer on the other, and that's about as good receiving as you can get, and we got the ball out to them pretty well, too. When we went up against the Colts in the Super Bowl, they ran their zone one way, doubling up on Maynard with two defensive backs, but Sauer was left one-on-one and he had a big day—eight catches. The next year we played the Colts and they were running "Double Double" pass defense, a zone where they double-covered both wide receivers, and since then all we've seen is more of the Double Double out of everybody. Every defense is out to take away the wide receivers. It's rough on the passing attack, and I'm afraid we were as much to blame as anybody.

Don Maynard, NFL's all-time receiver

What is the quarterback's job in the passing attack?

Our running attack may be fairly simple, if you can call anything simple in professional football, but we make up for it with our passing attack. Some people might call our passing theories complicated or confusing—I hope defensive people think so—but we like to think of ourselves as sophisticated. We have as many as 13 major variations off any one basic pattern, plus all the individual routes that I can call to go with that pattern, too. The patterns are timed so that different receivers make their cuts at different times, and a lot of the time the receivers have some options about which way they cut depending on the defense they see.

It might sound hard to handle, and I know a lot of teams don't try to do as much as we do, but we like it and we think we make it work pretty well. Defenses are leaving smaller and smaller holes to pass into, but we still get that son of a gun in there most of the time. It can get tough but we don't exactly get shut down ever.

How do you organize a passing attack?

The thought behind any pass pattern is to send out your receivers—the backs and ends— in such a way that you occupy most of the defensive people and leave one of your receivers basically covered by only one man. Say I'm going to throw deep down the sideline. If the defense has a free safety roaming around loose, I better be sure to call a pattern that sends out one of my receivers to try to keep that free safety busy. I have to give him something to do, somebody to cover, so he doesn't wander over to the sideline and bust up my deep pass. Or if I'm going to throw a hook to somebody, I have to occupy the linebacker who would otherwise be standing right in front of my receiver. I have to send a receiver —maybe a back—into that linebacker's area and make him move after that receiver so he gets the hell out of my way on the hook pass.

Occupying people is vital but it's not easy now that defenses are using so many different coverages. It's hard to know in advance who over there is responsible for what. You have to try to design pass patterns that are flexible enough to get somebody open no matter what defense they are playing, unless you can somehow get a line on what they're doing ahead of time.

What does "straddling the patterns" mean?

This has to do with the timing of your patterns. You have to straddle them, have the receivers make their final breaks one after the other rather than have them all turning around at once. If they all make that last cut at about the same time you can only check one guy. If he's covered and you turn to see somebody else, he's already made his cut and the defense has recovered to sew him up again.

If your receivers make their cuts one after the other, you check the first guy and if he's not open you move on to the second. If the defense has him covered as he cuts, you move on to the third, and so on. The pattern is spaced out and you have some time to move from one to another and find an open man. It's easiest, obviously, if the cuts come open right-to-left or left-to-right, so you can just pan across the field from one to another. This isn't always possible, but it is best if the last receiver makes his move over near the sideline. If he is not open by the time you get around to looking at him, you can take the ball and throw it the hell out of bounds.

How do the defenses dictate your passes?

Everything depends on what the other team is doing. As I say, you can't force the ball into a crowd. You can't go after the strength of a pass defense. You try to hit it where it is weak, find a place where one of your receivers is basically in a man-to-man situation with a defensive guy even if the defense is playing a zone.

To be able to do this, you have to understand all the various defenses and know where they are weak. Just like in the running game, this is no blackboard exercise. You can't tell everything from a diagram. You have to know about the people the other team is using as well as the defensive patterns they are using. A zone defense, for instance, is supposed to be tough to throw on deep. But maybe you know that a defensive guy in one of the deep zones just isn't too terribly fast. You might try to burn somebody by him even though you know he's coached to never let anybody get deep. Coaching and execution are two different things.

defensive coverages

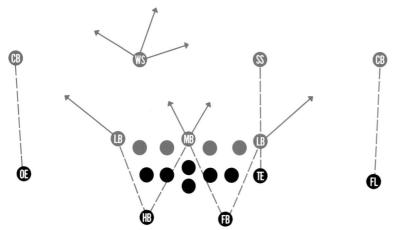

MAN-TO-MAN FREE—*The two cornerbacks (CB) cover the out end (OE) and flanker (FL). The strong safety (SS) covers the tight end (TE). The linebackers (LB, MB) divide up the halfback (HB) and fullback (FB). The weak safety (WS) moves anywhere he thinks help is needed.*

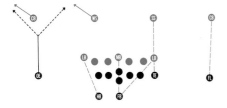

MAN-TO-MAN SPECIAL—*Same as above except weak safety helps cover the out end*

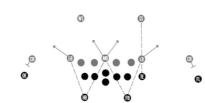

BUMP-AND-RUN—*cornerbacks line up close and bump receivers off course*

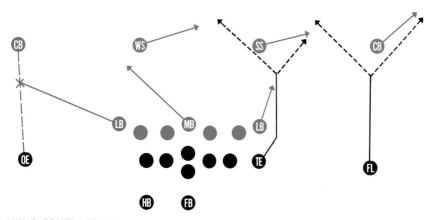

WING COVERAGE—*The weak safety crosses to opposite side and helps the strong safety and cornerback play inside-outside combination on tight end and flanker. The other cornerback gets help from his linebacker who comes out to ax the out end.*

MAN-TO-MAN

This is a defense that relies basically on the speed and reactions of the athletes involved. Three of the defensive backs are each assigned one of the offensive receivers, and they are asked to cover that receiver one-on-one wherever he goes. Since the receiver knows where he is going ahead of time, and the defensive man must react afterward, the offense has a definite advantage if the ball is thrown accurately and on time. In a basic version of the defense, the weak safety is "free"—he has no man to cover specifically—and he roams where needed, often watching the quarterback's eyes for clues. He is known as the "free safety." In another version of this defense, Man-to-Man Special, the weak safety helps the cornerback on his side double-covering on the "out end," the wide receiver on that side of the field.

WING COVERAGE

This is basically the reverse of Man-to-Man Special. Instead of helping the cornerback on his side, the weak safety runs to the opposite side and helps the strong safety and the other cornerback. The three defensive backs cover the two offensive receivers on that side, the tight end and the flanker, using various types of combinations. The cornerback on the other side is left alone with the out end, but he gets help from his linebacker. The linebacker runs out full steam and attempts to "ax" the out end, to knock him down and take him out of the play.

ZONE

In a zone defense the defensive backs and linebackers each covers an area of the field instead of trying to cover a specific pass receiver. In the basic zone defense, there are three deep zones covered by the two safeties and one cornerback, and four short zones, covered by the other cornerback and the three linebackers. A zone defense is tough for a quarterback to beat with a long pass because the players in the three deep zones are coached never to let a receiver get behind them. It can be hard on shorter passes, too, if the passer isn't sure exactly where the four short zone men are playing. If you watch your receiver instead of the defense, you can wind up throwing the ball right at one of the defensive men in the short zones. There are many different ways for the defense to divide up the seven zones and most teams use a lot of them to make it hard for the quarterback to tell which defensive player is responsible for what area of the field. Several of the variations are shown here.

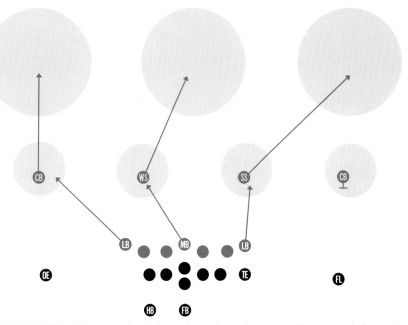

STRONG ZONE—*This is the basic four-short, three-deep zone. The two safeties and one cornerback each take a deep zone, and the three linebackers and the other cornerback each take a short zone.*

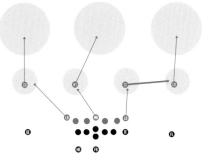

SAFETY X ZONE—*Strong safety crosses to short zone and cornerback goes deep*

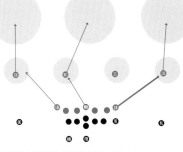

LINEBACKER X ZONE—*Linebacker crosses to outside zone, safety stays*

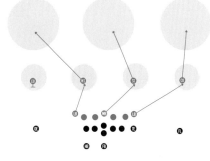

WEAK ZONE—*All assignments are the opposite of Strong Zone.*

WEAK SAFETY X ZONE—*Opposite of Safety X Zone; free safety takes short zone*

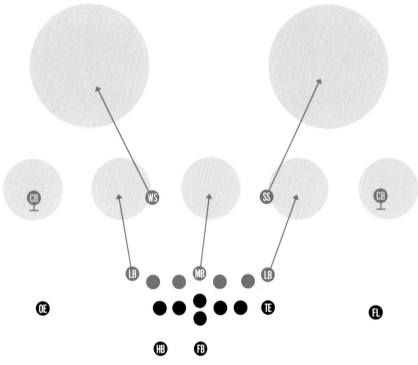

DOUBLE DOUBLE ZONE—*The two safeties divide and take two deep zones and the two cornerbacks and all three linebackers take the five short zones*

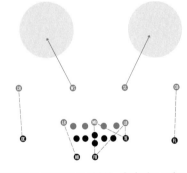

DOUBLE DOUBLE MAN—*Safeties take deep zones, cornerbacks take wide receivers, linebackers divide coverage of backs depending on backs' release.*

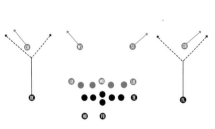

DOUBLE DOUBLE INSIDE OUTSIDE—*Safeties help cornerbacks on out end and flanker*

DOUBLE DOUBLE

The main idea of this defense is to double-cover both wide receivers and try to take them out of the passing attack. The two safeties split up, each going to help out the cornerback on his side covering the flanker and the out end. There are several varieties of the Double Double, but the main idea is that there are two men deep, the safeties, and five men short, the two cornerbacks and the three linebackers. With five men out there about ten to twenty yards, there is not much room to throw shorter passes like hooks and sidelines. For that reason, the defense is often used on third down and seven or more. It is also hard to throw deep on the Double Double because the two safeties pick up the two wide receivers and the linebacker attempts to keep the tight end from getting out fast enough to catch a deep pass. The defense is most effective in sure passing situations, when the linebackers can run back full speed into their areas. If it is used in a running situation and the offense fakes a run, the linebackers can be frozen up near the line looking at the fake and not get back fast enough to cover their assignments.

BLITZ

Getting the passer is still the best pass defense and that's the basic idea behind the Blitz. One, two or all three linebackers will rush the passer and sometimes they are even joined by a safety. The usual four-man pass rush can suddenly become eight in an all-out Blitz. Blitzing is a gambling type of defense, counting on surprise to disrupt the offense and dump the passer. If the linebackers Blitz, the defensive backs are left alone in the coverage so there aren't enough people to play zone defenses. They play Man-to-Man, often a little tighter than usual because they don't figure the quarterback will be able to stand up long enough to throw a long pass and they don't want to get beat quickly before the Blitz can take effect.

FIVE BACKS

More and more defenses are adjusting their personnel to fit the situation, just as the quarterback calls his plays to fit the situation. In passing situations these days, many coaches are taking out a linebacker—who is a bigger, slower guy who can play against runs well—and replacing him with a fast defensive back. This gives the defense five fast people to cover our three main receivers, the flanker, tight end and out end. We could try to run against this defense but on third and ten, for instance, the odds are against us getting the ten yards on the ground. With the five backs and two remaining linebackers, the defense can play various combinations of Zone and Man-to-Man.

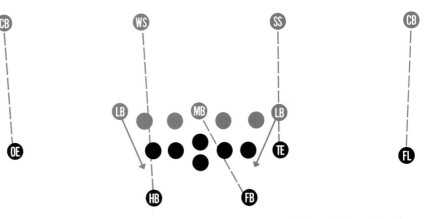

BLITZ—When the two outside backers blitz, the rest of the defense is forced to play straight Man-to-Man, not a good situation if pass is made

FREE SAFETY BLITZ—All-out pass rush, defensive end helps cover halfback

STRONG SAFETY BLITZ—Harder version because free safety must try to come across and cover tight end

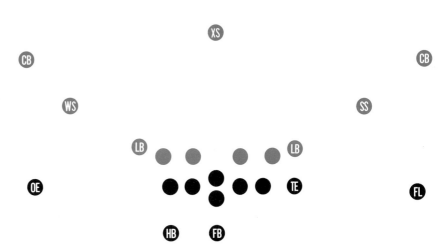

FIVE BACKS—One linebacker comes out and an extra defensive back comes in to give more pass coverage in sure passing situations

171

reading the defense

To throw the ball in this league you need an arm, no doubt about that. You've got to be able to put that ball out there. No bloopers allowed.

But as much as a good arm, you've got to have good eyes. You have to be able to "read" the defense, not just look at them, but read them—decode what they're doing and get some sort of meaning just like you decode written words and get a meaning. "If the safety goes here, and the linebacker goes there, then back over here my guy will be in this open place"—it works like that except there's no time to think about it. You thought about it at one point in time, back in training camp or out at practice, but on the field it just has to happen right now.

Not too many guys read defenses knowledgeably. You hear a lot about how quarterbacks are running more these days. Sure they're running. If you can't find anybody to throw to, you better run. And if you can't read the defense—look out there and recognize their pattern, realize which of your guys is open—you won't find too many people open to throw.

What is the goal of reading defenses?

What I try to do as I drop into the pocket is find a receiver who is covered man-to-man by one guy, or at least the situation which is the most like that. Even though teams are playing so much zone, a defensive guy isn't going to just stand there in the center of his zone and watch us complete a pass five yards from where he's standing. He's going to go over to cover the guy. So

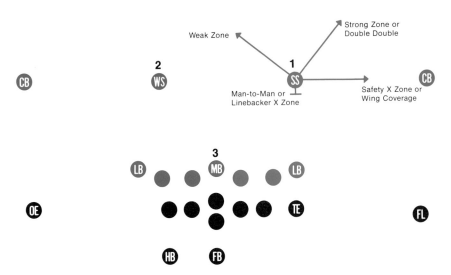

Often the first man I read is the strong safety. What he does will usually give me a good clue to the entire defense. Then I will check the weak safety and middle backer to complete the read.

what I'm trying to do is find some part of the defense where one of the defensive people is left alone with a big zone to cover and one of my guys can get in there and work on him man-to-man.

There's no way I can count on which receiver that's going to be before the play starts. I may be thinking about trying to throw to my right flanker but when the play starts, all five of my guys are primary receivers. I have to find the one who is basically one-on-one versus whatever defense I see. If they rotate a zone out to my right, I'm coming off that flanker right now and going back to my left, back where the cornerman has been left pretty much alone with my other wide receiver. However if he can get help with some good linebacker coverage it's mighty difficult. The linebacker plays a

major role in pass coverage.

How do you read a defense?

You have to look. Look and see what's happening. In some ways it's just that simple, even though I know some guys *don't* look. There's a lot going on in your head, about steps and timing and finding your receiver and those defensive linemen making trouble, but you have to get all that together and look out there anyway. You have to see what's going on.

Usually if I can see two or three guys over on defense, they'll tell me what is going on everyplace. The most important man to check, most of the time, is the strong safety and that's pretty convenient because he's easy to see. The strong safety lines up over the tight end and he's only maybe ten yards away from me when the play starts. Most of the time, against a majority of teams, the first move the strong safety makes will tell me a lot about the basic coverage.

After checking the strong safety it depends on the play but

usually I'll check the weak safety and the middle linebacker. Those are the three guys in the center of their defense and whatever pattern they show me, the rest of the defense should be following. If the two safeties both start the same way deep, it's a Zone. If they divide deep, it's Double Double. If the weak safety moves to the strong side and the middle linebacker goes weak, it's Wing coverage.

I see this movement—"read" it —in the first instant after the snap, on my first step back or maybe my second on some plays. And as I see what they're doing, my mind is racing on to the next step—who can I throw to out there? Who's going to be one-on-one? Or which linebacker can we work on best?

How do defenses try to confuse a quarterback?

The more weeks and years defenses play their various zones, the better they get at hiding what they're doing. On some teams, for instance, the strong safety doesn't go tearing deep to the corner just because that's going to be his zone. If he can see a receiver headed for that area, he'll take off. But if he sees his zone isn't immediately threatened—maybe I'm not sending anybody toward that zone or maybe his cornerback knocks my flanker down and keeps him from getting deep, the safety will "hang," or "float," and wait on developments. That makes him hard to read. If he doesn't move for his zone, I'm not sure what zone he's covering.

On the good teams these days, the people playing zones are trying to float as long as they can. They don't make a neat zone pattern any more, and it's hard to read a muddled pattern.

Another thing these people do is hide. They line up in places where you think they couldn't possibly cover the zone they're assigned to. The strong safety may come up near the line although he's supposed to cover a deep zone. The fact is he *can't* cover that deep zone from where he lines up, not if we go right after him, but he's counting on the fact that I see him up short. He's hoping I won't pick on him in the deep zone because I'd never dream he was going to have to cover it. And he's right, sometimes.

What's the next step after reading the coverage?

I can't let my mind get lazy out there. Just because I've read the coverage, just because I know a receiver should be getting open, I can't stop looking and reading. Maybe I've got a deep sideline pass called to a wide receiver, and on my first step I read that their defense will be all right for that pattern. I can't stop there. Maybe something easier is going to happen. Throwing a deep sideline is a tough pass. Maybe the way their defense is breaking, my tight end will come open over the center for a shorter pass or my fullback will be able to swing into a seam. Hell, I know I've got the deep sideline if I need it. I've got to keep on looking for something better.

Can you read a defense before the play starts?

You can't, always. You can't always be sure of what they're going to run until the play starts. Sometimes you can, though, and other times you can tell at least what they *won't* run.

When I come up to the line, I look all over that defense. I check everybody, looking for something that will help me. Sometimes you can see by where a guy lines up what he's going to do. If the strong safety is going to take the deep sideline zone, sometimes he has to cheat out that way a little bit. Or maybe I can see a cornerman up a little closer than usual and just a little inside my receiver. That could mean the linebackers are going to blitz me. If they blitz they take away any help the cornerman might have to his inside. That's why he's cheated in a little, to take the inside move away from my flanker. A defense can be hurt badly on a short inside slant if the blitz is on.

Reading at the line like this is something that comes with experience. After you've been standing up at the line for twenty-three years, you begin to get a feel for things. You see somebody looking a little strange and you can pick up on what he's going to do. Sometimes a linebacker will be standing out there trying to look real casual, just sort of standing straight up and maybe looking to the outside mostly. But every now and then he'll cut his eyes in at me, glance in quick, and then go on looking casual. He's coming. He's going to blitz me. I can just sense it.

Of course, sometimes he doesn't. They're getting paid to think, too.

Or sometimes I can tell a back is going to play man-to-man or zone by the way he's standing before the play starts. If he's kind of hunched over pretty good, tight, poised, and really staring at the receiver in front of him, I might get the idea that he's going to play man-to-man on that guy. But maybe he's more relaxed out there, standing looser, looking at me more than at his receiver. That looks like he isn't too concerned with one man. He's probably going to play zone.

None of this is foolproof, but it helps. A lot of times I can pick something up and call an audible to take advantage. There was one play in an exhibition game where I got caught after I had already audibled but at least I didn't throw an interception. I came up and saw the cornerman standing real deep so I audibled to a quick sideline pass to my flanker. But then I looked at the safety on that side. He looked a little tense. His feet were slightly open, like he was thinking of sprinting into that deep zone behind the cornerman. If he did that, the cornerman would come racing up, and he might run right into my quick pass and step down the sideline for six points.

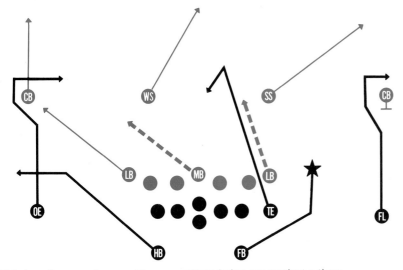

This is a diagram of a versatile pass pattern being run against a three-deep zone defense. Even after I see the safeties go into their deep zones, I have to read the linebackers (heavy dotted lines). If the strong-side backer and middle backer go left, I can throw right to my fullback.

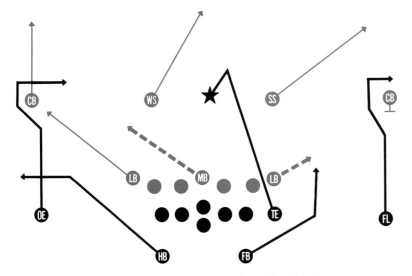

This is the same play against the same basic defense, but this time the strong-side linebacker decides to play the fullback and the middle backer still goes left, so I throw to my tight end in the middle.

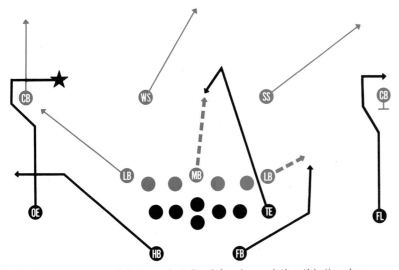

Again the same play and defense, but the defensive variation this time has the strong-side and middle backers favoring the right side so I come around to my left and throw to my out end.

I wasn't sure about that safety, but he did look a little strange.

My snap count was two, so when I said the first "Hut" I really hollered it out. Overemphasized it. Sure enough, that safety flinched. He started back into the deep zone. I took the ball on the second count and, boy, I just threw that thing into the stands. I couldn't change the play by then but I wasn't going to let the cornerman have it.

What happens if you get too excited?

You can get yourself moving too quick, do something before you've checked everything out. I did that to myself one Thanksgiving Day. It was the last two minutes. I was on the sidelines and Weeb was saying, "All right, get together, get together, get a play." So we hurried up and got together and got a play and ran out on the field and went right from the line. I dropped back fast looking to my right and the coverage they had took away all my receivers over there, so I whipped around expecting my receiver on the left to be open breaking inside. But the linebacker was slowing him, bump-and-run, and I was too quick. I was starting to throw already as I came around and I saw my receiver hung up but I couldn't get the ball back. I tried, but it just flopped out there. The linebacker got it. That's a bad feeling. You've got to be quick, but you can't be too quick. I got to hurrying when we were calling the play and I just kept on hurrying as I threw the ball. You can't let that happen. You have to keep your mind under control.

MAN-TO-MAN

As I say, designing a pass offense you not only call plays against the defense you are seeing, but also against the people playing that defense. This is easiest to do against a team which plays a lot of Man-to-Man. If you know which is their weakest man, you can try to pick on him with individual patterns by the receiver he is covering. Just go out and fake the guy and beat him. In fact, a good receiver should be able to get some kind of open against almost any defensive back who is covering him one-on-one. The way our pass offense is designed, we have a great deal of flexibility in how to get our different receivers running different routes. We have basic overall patterns involving all our receivers, a number of overall variations on each of these patterns, and a great number of individual routes that I can tell one or two guys to run off the overall patterns. If I see a Man-to-Man, we are set up so I can call virtually anything I want to any of our receivers.

1. The strong safety is playing Man (large circle) and the weak safety is heading away. so it's Man-to-Man Special. 2. I've got problems (small circle) but Richard is one-on-one. 3. The cornerback is occupied with the flanker in front of him (large circle) and Caster breaks behind him. 4. Richard makes a great catch and there's no one there to help the safety.

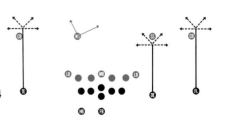

Offense can run slot formation with both wide receivers on one side and run various types of combinations

WING COVERAGE

If the defense runs a Wing Coverage, with the weak safety running across to the other side of the field, the easiest thing to do is throw back to the side he left where the cornerback is left covering the out end man-to-man. The linebacker on that side runs out and tries to block the out end, but if we avoid him, we can run any kind of pattern we want on that one cornerback. But just because they are running a combination coverage over on our strong side, where the tight end and flanker are, doesn't mean we can't throw over there. We can run a combination pattern, too, having our receivers cross, or fake a cross, and then see if the defensive backs get confused about which receiver they should cover. Occasionally one of our receivers gets left all alone while two of their guys cover one of ours. And most times we wind up with at least one of the receivers man-to-man on one back. It's just something I have to read right. If I can see what they're doing and throw it quickly, we can usually get something. If I read it wrong, however, there are a lot of people over there to get in the way.

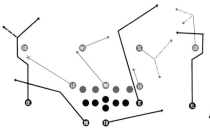

If out end escapes linebacker he has one man to beat; combination on other side depends on which defensive back tries to cover which of the receivers

1. *With the free safety in the middle (top circle) and the strong safety up some and outside (bottom circle) it looks like either Safety X Zone or Wing.* **2.** *It's Wing, as the free safety starts over but the strong safety plays Man.* **3.** *The flanker and tight end run a combination pattern and the backs get momentarily confused.* **4.** *The ball is just on time.*

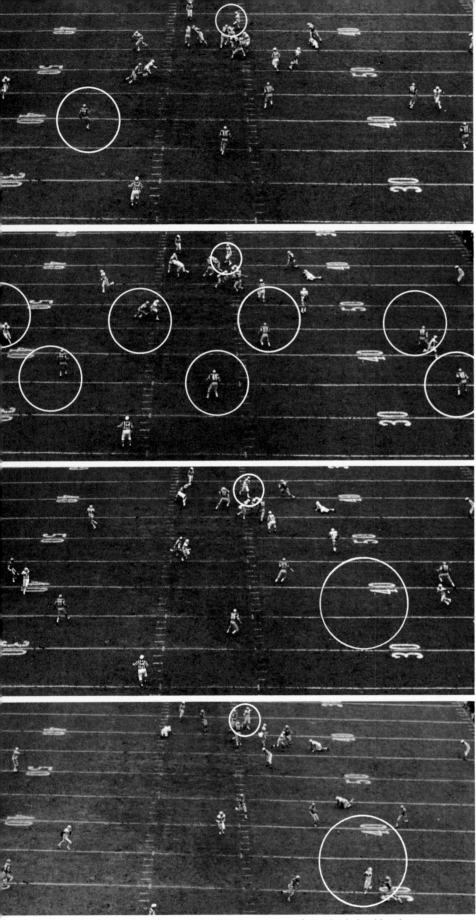

ZONE

1 The basic way to attack a zone is to go away from the side where the defense is leaving a back up in a short zone. On the other side, where both the cornerback and the safety are dropping off into deep zones, the linebacker on that side has to run back into the short zone and since he is between me and my receiver, he can't watch us both at once. We can often work something like a hook in his area and underneath those two deep backs. If the backs start to cheat

2 up close to stop those shorter passes, sometimes you can burn them by going deep. Another way to go after a Zone is to flood certain areas of it with an overload of receivers. Even though a defensive man is playing in a certain zone, he will still go after a receiver who comes into his zone rather than just waiting around. But if you send one receiver into his zone short and another deep, he doesn't know which way to go. Whichever receiver he tries to cover, we

3 throw to the other one. The main thing on this type of pattern is that the blocking hold up to give the quarterback a chance to find the open man.

1. I drop back (small circle) reading the strong safety who is backing into a deep zone. 2. As I come around I see it is a Strong Zone—four short and three deep—so I look for my out end breaking in. 3. Eddie Bell makes his cut, heading for the empty seam between zones (large circle), and I throw at the same time. 4. The ball approaches just ahead of the defense.

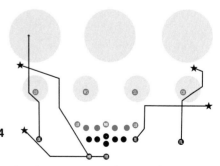

Another way to attack a zone is to flood the short outside zones and throw to whichever receiver is open

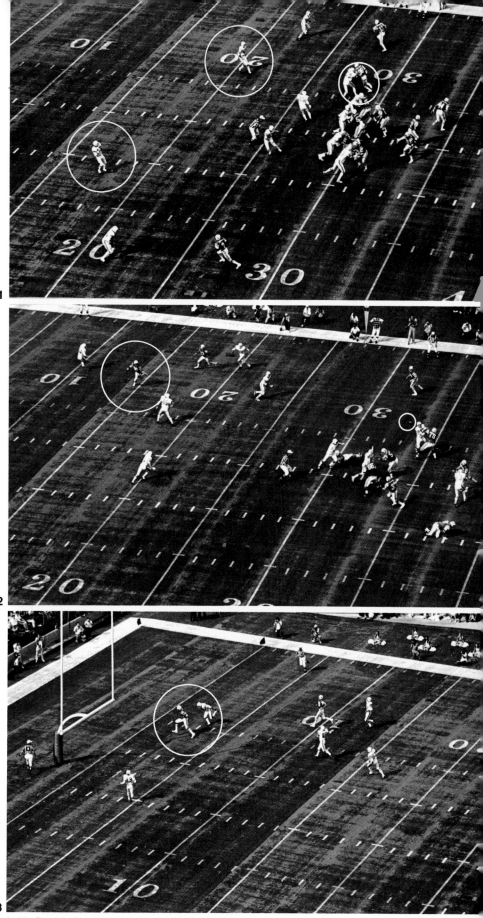

DOUBLE DOUBLE

The big beautiful hole in a Double Double defense is right in the center deep. The two safeties split up, each going to his own side of the field, and they leave a big gap in between. They are counting on two facts. First, they hope that the offense won't be able to adjust its play after the snap to take advantage of the hole. Second, the linebacker who lines up over the tight end usually tries to hold him up and keep him from getting out deep. On the Jets, we have an automatic reaction on most patterns if we see a Double Double. Our tight end, Richard Caster, will break his pattern and head for the center if he sees the Double Double happening and if I read it too, we can get some easy yards. But both of us have to pick it up. Another idea against the Double Double is to flood the sidelines short and deep. Usually the safeties aren't too quick to run all the way to the sidelines because they are a little concerned about the middle. So the cornerback has to cover the sidelines and if he covers the deep receiver we throw to the shorter one and vice versa.

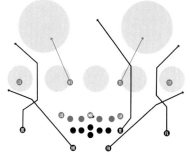

Best chance against Double Double is to hit tight end deep in middle; also possible to flood short outside zones

1. *It's Double Double as the two safeties split up to cover two deep zones (large circles). Tight end Richard Caster (small circle) escapes his linebacker.* **2.** *Richard reads the defense and breaks for the hole in the middle.* **3.** *He has the ball before the safeties converge.*

BLITZ

1 There are two basic ways to handle the Blitz. First, you can keep your backs in to block the blitzing linebackers. The defensive backs are left downfield covering man-to-man and if nobody gets in to the quarterback, somebody should get open downfield. This is usually what we do on the Jets. Our backs are good blockers and teams don't usually want to leave our receivers man-to-man because we beat that pretty good. The other way to handle the Blitz is to run **2** a "Blitz Control"—the back or the tight end who would normally block a specific blitzing linebacker instead runs a quick pattern and the quarterback flips him the ball before the blitzer can get to him. On patterns where we are sending out both backs, somebody is always designated the "Blitz Control" and if a Blitz shows, he looks right now and I get the ball to him. If a safety is blitzing, the wide receiver on that side should see it and slant right into the hole **3** the safety vacates. This is the play George Sauer ran a couple of times in the 1969 Super Bowl when the Baltimore Colts sent their safety on a blitz.

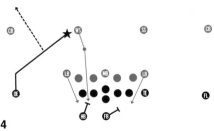

4

If safety blitzes, out end should automatically slant in; or have him fake in and then head for the corner

1. *The linebacker is blitzing but I dump the ball out to my fullback, John Riggins, who is the Blitz Control.* **2.** *With no linebacker to beat, Riggins heads for the little backs.* **3.** *He is by one and going over the second.* **4.** *He goes out at the five. A powerful runner is ideal for blitz control.*

PLAY ACTION

One way to go after any type of pass defense is to use play action —that is, fake a running play and then pass. A good running fake will usually hold the linebackers and keep them from getting into their pass coverage. They have to wait to see if the play is a run before they drop back. Some teams use a lot of play action and we use it part of the time, too. But there is a definite problem with play action, which is that you can't read pass coverages very well. I usually see what the defense is doing on my first or second step back from center, but if on that first and second step I'm involved with making a fake handoff, by the time I turn around to see the defense, things are pretty confusing. Maybe the weak safety is only five feet ten inches. I know he's out there, but where? If I can't find him, or whomever I have to check, it can start getting dangerous to throw the ball. We read defenses well— my receivers as well as myself— and we adjust well to what they are doing, so we tend to use more dropback passes and just try to beat their coverages instead of attempting to fake them out with play action. But we do use play action some, and it can be very effective for us.

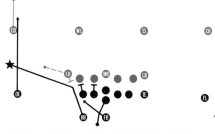

Fullback fakes off tackle, halfback fakes block on linebacker; linebacker must come up and halfback slips open on outside where linebacker should be

1. *On the play following the one on page 180, Clifton McLain and I start to fake a handoff.* **2.** *I hide the ball away and my tight end, Wayne Stewart starts out while the safety covering him is still looking at the fake.* **3.** *The safety sees his mistake, but Stewart is gone.* **4.** *Things should only be this easy all the time as Stewart prepares for a touchdown.*

getting it together

It's hard work getting ready to play but it's better than the losing feeling

I talked earlier about how a passer has to build himself up by stages. Every year I go back to the basics about throwing the ball and work the whole throwing motion up from the bottom. There's no way I can expect to go out on the first day of camp and move and throw the way I was moving and throwing the previous winter after six months of working at it.

The same thing holds true for the mind. I have to gear my mind up, work it up in stages, the same way I do my body. When I start each season, my mind isn't used to moving the way it does as a football player. I've been doing some other things, using my head in different ways, and when we start working in the summer I have to begin pulling my mind together for the job at hand. It's not an easy thing to do, having all the things I need to run the team ready in my mind—all the things about which plays from which formations against which defenses, and reading defenses and running audibles and working the snap count and staying on top of the flow of the game.

I realized this especially in 1971 when I went back to play late in the year after missing most of the season with an injured knee. I only worked with the team one week and then I was back in there and it was like being in a fire drill. A bunch of stuff was happening out there and I was just sort of hanging on and doing the best I could.

Any time of the year I can go out and run a team and run some basic plays, but when it comes to reading strong safety, weak safety, middle guard, going from there to one receiver to another to another—having my head together like that takes some time.

How does your mind feel at the start of the year?

That first or second game in the summer especially, my mind is moving a little slow. I go up to the line and I see something but I'm not really sure about it. It looks like there's something there I could take but hell, the play I've already called in the huddle still looks pretty good and I just let it slide, go on with the play I've got called. Say it's second and four or something and I've got a running play on. I come out to the line and see something to throw at. Why stick my fool head out? Just go ahead with the run. It's like I'm shying away a little. I'm not going strong, having confidence in what I see.

How do you work your head into shape?

The goal is to get my mind geared up to where it is running fast enough, to where everything just goes click-click-click. I have to have my mind together so I know what I want to call, know all the adjustments I'd have to make on the play, and still have enough space and time in my mind to go up to the line and observe and think. Wait a minute, something's moving differently out there. Boom! Jump on it. Change the play to get the percentages the most in my favor.

It's something I have to practice during the summer, think about thinking, keep my mind going just like it does in a game. As the exhibition season goes on, things start falling back in place. In the second game of 1972 there was one play I remember specifically. I came out and had a run called, but I saw where they were in Man-to-Man. I had been looking at defenses and calling audibles all week, getting my mind ready, and I wasn't going to let that Man-to-Man go by. So I checked to a play that sent my tight end short to the outside and my flanker on that side down and angling in. I was feeling pretty good and threw to my flanker, but the damn cornerman stepped right in and picked the ball off. See the thing is, that cornerman was a ten-year veteran. He knows enough that if he sees the tight end start to the outside, he expects the flanker to come to the inside into the vacant area. He just shot in there like a bullet and burned me.

My mind wasn't up to that stage yet. I wasn't thinking about who the people were that were playing the defense, I was just thinking about the type of defense. It all comes in stages. By the time the season begins, one of the things I write down in my scouting report is the number of years each defensive

guy has played. Later in the year, I'd have been thinking about the fact that the cornerman was an old head and I would have called something different— maybe send the tight end out and have the flanker fake in and then go out to the corner, play on the fact that the cornerman would be expecting an inside move.

It just takes time. I usually need about five or six weeks of practice and about four games before I've got my mind going at the speed I want.

How does it feel when you're mind is moving right?

It's a good feeling. You're really working then, running smooth. You're getting after something the way you're supposed to be, taking the defense apart where it's weak.

I believe you've got to be quick out there. Your throw has to be quick and your mind has to be quick. If you're too relaxed and lackadaisical about things, you sort of ease into them rather than jumping right on.

Do you have to work to psyche yourself up for games?

Psyching yourself is another part of getting your mind ready. It's just as important as getting to where you can do all the things quickly. Of course, some weeks I don't have to worry about psyching myself. It doesn't take much doing to get myself ready for Miami, say, or Oakland. But there's 14 games in a season and some weeks I just don't feel that same energy flowing and that's when I have to work on myself, keep myself pushing.

I have to go over the situation in my mind and convince myself of the importance of the game. In the first place, it doesn't matter who we're playing. Any team we face is good enough to beat us or else they wouldn't be playing professionally. Then I think about the end of the year. When you look at records of the top teams there's usually only a half game or a game separating them. Every game matters, every week counts the same. You've got to *know* that, get it into your mind, and think of what kind of a feeling it would be if you got to the end of the year and lost by one game where you didn't really work hard enough.

And then not even thinking about the championship, it's just such a bad feeling to lose. I mean I'm not crazy competitive. I don't mind losing so much when I'm shooting pool or playing basketball with my friends. But football, that's my job. That's the main thing. And losing feels terrible. It's not just my feelings, but everybody else on the team, players and coaches and everybody. And when I come home my friends are all down. And I call up my family and they're upset. It's just a down scene, losing. It's pretty tough to enjoy yourself much during the week if you blew the game on Sunday.

So if I'm feeling early in the week like I'm having trouble getting up and concentrating, I spend some time thinking about these things and I get in there

and do what I've got to do.

Do you want to feel excited during the game?

I've thought a lot about that. There have been some times when I've worried about being too nonchalant or lackadaisical during a game. When I'm playing I'm usually pretty matter-of-fact, just going about the business. And I've asked myself, Why? How come I'm not driving? How come I'm not excited?

But the thing I've decided is that I've just been in a lot of games. I've seen a lot of situations and I've had to handle a lot of problems and by now most of it is second nature to me. It's not new stuff, nothing where I have to worry about whether I can handle the circumstances. And I'm not a very excitable person anyway. So where a couple of years ago I might be telling myself, "Come on, Joe, get yourself revved up," now I feel like it's all right.

I don't think being excited helps a quarterback anyway. When I say I want to be psyched up every week, I'm talking about practicing and concentrating all week. I don't mean I want to be jumping up and down on the field on Sunday. I've got a lot of head work to do out there and I don't think that being excited helps that especially. I know I didn't like all the hoopla and cheering back in college and getting all worked up over what I had to do. Maybe guys in other positions, it helps them to be

charging full speed. But I think a quarterback needs to be pretty calm to do what he has to do. But remember, don't let being calm detract from your confidence.

Do you miss the excitement?

I get excited enough, in a way. It's always fun to move that ball, to drive down the field and get it in the end zone. That's your goal, and that always feels good.

But talking about the nervous excitement, I don't miss that at all. If I think about how I feel before a game, I know that's a bad feeling. Jeez, that's awful, moving around and you can't sit still and you're feeling sick. I'm glad that feeling leaves me. I get worked up before a game, but when it's time to go to work it's all business, and that calm sets in. Just, boom! and your head's right there. You're thinking about what you have to do and forgetting all that other stuff. And I think that's good. I know it's good.

Don't you get upset during a game?

I'll get ticked off sometimes, if somebody blows an assignment or something. I'll let people know how I feel. Sometimes the referees will miss something really bad, and I think they ought to hear about it. Hell, it's their job and if they don't do their job right, they're affecting my whole team.

But I can get angry and let it out and then just go right on with business. I step into the huddle and there's a new situation like any other time. That's the key. As long as I'm reacting right, I've got my head in the right place.

The same thing goes for the times when I make a bad play. Any time I throw an interception or call a really bad play or screw up something like that, it really works on my head for a while. But you can't let it get to you. You've got to be able to go right back and be able to attack it with an all-out confident approach, with your full thrust. You have to go about your job full speed without having any qualms about it.

Even if you just screwed up, you need confidence in your ability mentally and physically to do the job. I've played a lot of football. I know I can do it. Anytime in any profession mistakes or errors are made. What you do when that happens is find out what exactly happened and why it happened. Then you're better prepared for a similar situation. Let's not make the same mistake twice. So I figure it out and then I just go back to work. Even though it still ticks me off and I still come back to it throughout the course of the game when I'm on the sideline or whatever. How could I do that? But when it's time to play I just say, "Forget it, buddy. Let's go."

I have to be able to do that because a quarterback has to keep his mind functioning well. You have to go through the stages and get your mind together through weeks and months of practice, and then you have to keep it together out on the field.

No matter how long you play it's still great to score points and win games

appendix

EQUIPMENT

What you wear to protect yourself in a game as rough as football is obviously very important, and I don't think some guys give enough thought to the problem.

I wear some equipment that other quarterbacks don't, especially the three-bar face mask and a set of rib pads, not to mention all the metal I'm carrying around on my knees. Sometimes I'm asked why I wear all that equipment and my answer is pretty simple: Why not?

Take the hinged metal bar I have on the outside of my right knee. It occurred to me early in the 1972 season that I really hadn't been hit on that knee in years. But in the Monday night game in Oakland, I took a crack on the outside of that knee that like to stove it in. When I got up I had a sprained ankle, not a torn knee. The metal brace had held all right and the shock apparently got transferred to my ankle. I don't enjoy sprained ankles any but they're better than another knee operation.

But not everybody has bad knees. The rib pads are more important for a healthy quarterback. A passer is always getting hit with his arm in the air and his body exposed. It's awfully easy to get cracked ribs, or even ribs that are just badly bruised, and either type of injury is enough to keep you from throwing the ball much. In the last few years I can think of a time when

Bart Starr missed a lot of one season with bad ribs and Johnny Unitas got knocked out of the Super Bowl in 1971 when George Andrie busted him in the side. It seems to me rib pads are just a sensible thing to wear when you know you're going to get hit like that.

I'm even more convinced about the three-bar cage on my helmet. I started wearing it after I broke my cheek bone. Some guy came up under my mask with his forearm and knocked my whole helmet off. After that I went to the linebacker's face mask with three bars. It curves down and under your chin a little and a guy can't get under it.

I just don't see why you shouldn't take the extra protection. It doesn't hurt your vision any. You aren't looking down at your chin anyway. In practice I've even worn the lineman's mask that has a bar coming down between the eyes and that doesn't keep me from seeing either.

There's some guys around the league who use only one-bar masks. We've got a couple on our team and I tell them they're crazy. It's ridiculous running around like that. It's suicide. And there's no reason for it that has to do with playing any better. The only reason people wear a one-bar mask is because they want to look like somebody wearing a one-bar mask.

Now when you talk about shoulder pads on a quarterback, you're talking about something different altogether. A quarterback can't wear maximum pads

on his shoulders because he has to have free movement to throw the ball. That's the way I choose shoulder pads—because they're comfortable and don't bother me throwing.

The way I fall, there's not much strain on my shoulders anyway. I try to go down forward on my hands or straight backward on my back. I try never to fall sideways on my arm and shoulder because every time this happens to me it hurts. And if you fall wrong on your shoulder, you're going to get it separated no matter what kind of pad you're wearing.

So I don't need much shoulder pad. I've worn the same pair ever since I've been with the Jets. I picked out a really light pair and then cut off the top flap of padding and there really isn't too much left at all. I suppose any kid would look at those pads and call them band-aids. You look at them and they're decrepit. They're held together with tape and everything. They've really got no class at all—*except* if you know what they've been through. Then they've got all the class in the world.

Everything I wear on the field, I've given a lot of thought to. A quarterback has to be careful the way he dresses. You're standing out there a sitting duck for some pretty big people, so it just makes sense to wear anything that might help you survive.

When the linebackers start to arrive, rib pads and a three-bar cage seem to be pretty sensible equipment

GLOSSARY

Audible
A play hollered by the quarterback at the line of scrimmage just before the snap

Backpedal
Quarterback retreats to pass by backing up while facing square downfield

Blitz
Linebackers or defensive backs rush the passer

Bomb
A long pass

Bump-and-run
A type of pass defense where the cornerbacks, and sometimes the strong safety, come up on the line of scrimmage and shove the receiver as the play starts to break up the timing of a pass play

Check off
See "Audibles"

Check-with-me
The quarterback says this rather than call a play in the huddle and then takes the team to the line and calls an audible

Combination coverage
Two or more defensive backs combine to cover two or more receivers using variations like inside-outside or short-and-long

Cornerbacks
The two defensive backs stationed wide to cover the wide receivers for the offense

Count
See "Snap count"

Counterplay
A play that begins as if it were one play and then develops into another, usually hitting toward the opposite side of the defense

Criss-cross
Offensive linemen make an "X" move to each block the other's defensive man; pass receivers cross each other's routes; has other meanings also

Cut
A sharp change of direction

Delay
A short pass pattern run after faking a block for a second or two

Draw
A run that begins as a fake pass; the quarterback slips the runner the ball during his dropback to pass; hopefully the defensive linemen are drawn in by the fake pass and overrun the ball carrier

Double coverage
Defensive pass coverage assigning two players to cover one pass receiver

Double Double
A pass defense where each safety helps the cornerback on his side double cover the wide receiver on that side

Dropback
A quarterback's retreat to pass

Field position
The yard-line, or general proximity to either goal line, where the ball is put in play; "good" or "bad" field position affects tactical thinking

Flanker
The wide receiver for the offense on the side where the tight end lines up.

Flood pattern
A pass pattern where two or more receivers overload one area of the defense

Formation
The alignment of the offensive players before the play begins

Game plan
The list of plays and the strategic and tactical thinking that a team takes into each game.

Grip
The position of the hand on the ball ready for passing

Handoff
Hand-to-hand exchange of the ball from the quarterback to a ball carrier

Hook pattern
An offensive receiver runs downfield, stops, and moves back slightly toward the passer

Interception
A defensive player catches a pass

Individual route (or pattern)
One of many pass patterns run by a single pass receiver while the rest of the receivers run a pre-arranged pattern in concert

Influence blocking
Blocking which is deliberately designed *not* to open the hole where the play is intended to go on the theory that the defenders will react against the blocking pattern they see and leave the desired hole unguarded by themselves

Isolate
The offense maneuvers to get one pass receiver running against only one defensive player

Key
Each defensive player has one or several offensive players he watches; the first moves of those players is the "key" to what the defensive player should do

Key breaker
An offensive tactic where some or all of the offensive players make moves that are usually associated with one play, but then another play is run; confuses the defensive keys

Man-to-Man
A defensive pass coverage where each defensive back is assigned one pass receiver to cover individually

Middle guard
The middle linebacker

Move
A spontaneous or pre-planned fake or cut by a pass receiver or a ball carrier to get away from a defender

Out end
The wide receiver for the offense on the side away from the tight end

Outlet
A pass receiver designated as the man to throw to if everything else fails or the passer is rushed

Overshift
The defensive line lines up unbalanced toward the strong side of the offensive

Pass coverage
The defensive maneuvers to cover the offensive pass receivers

Passing lanes
Natural "corridors" between defensive people through which a pass can be thrown

Pass pattern
The pre-arranged design of the routes the offensive receivers take to get open to catch passes

Pickoff pass
A pass play where one offensive receiver "accidentally" gets in the way of a defender trying to cover another pass receiver

Pocket
The small area which the offensive blockers attempt to keep clear of defensive rushers where the quarterback stands to throw the ball

Primary receiver
The receiver most likely to come open on a specific pass pattern against a specific defense

Pull
An offensive lineman moves sideways to trap or move out around end

Reading
The quarterback watches the first moves of the defensive backs and linebackers after the snap to determine what type of pass coverage the defense is using

Release
The action of the arm and hand at the time the ball leaves the fingertips

Rotate
If both safeties start deep in the same direction in a four-short, three-deep zone, the zone is said to "rotate" in that direction

Sack
The tackling of the quarterback before he can pass

Scouting
Advance work to determine the capabilities and weaknesses of your upcoming opponents

Screen
A deceptive pass that is thrown after a delay to a back who has a screen of offensive linemen in front of him to block for him

Seam
An open area between defensive people into which an offensive receiver can go to catch passes

Short drop
A short retreat to pass by the quarterback, only three or five steps instead of seven, used on quick passes

Sideline pattern
An offensive receiver runs downfield and breaks square toward the sideline

Signals
The offensive or defensive play-calling system; the words and numbers called by the quarterback at the line of scrimmage

Single coverage
Man-to-Man coverage

Slant
An offensive receiver runs downfield and angles in toward the middle

Slot formation
An offensive formation with both wide receivers lined up on the same side and away from the tight end

Snap
The exchange of the ball from the center to the quarterback through the center's legs that begins each play

Snap count
The pre-arranged number on which the ball will be snapped

Strong side
The side of the offensive formation where the tight end is lined up

Strong zone
A zone defense where both safeties move deep toward the strong side of the offensive formation

Sucker play
A running play where an offensive lineman goes one way, to fool the defensive lineman in front of him into following, and the runner goes through the resulting hole

Tight end
An eligible pass receiver for the offense who lines up tight to the other linemen and carries a big share of the blocking

Trap
An offensive lineman pulls sideways and hits a defensive lineman from the side as the defensive lineman crosses the line of scrimmage

Turnover
The offense loses the ball to the defense by a fumble or interception

Weak safety
One of the two safeties for the defense; a defensive back who lines up on the side away from the tight end; usually fast and quick reacting

Weak side
The side of the offensive formation where the tight end is not lined up

Weak zone
A zone defense where the two safeties both move deep toward the weak side of the offensive formation

Wide receivers
Offensive pass receivers lined up far from the ball and the other players (out end and flanker)

Wing Coverage
A pass defense where the weak safety goes to the strong side to help the strong safety and cornerback in a combination coverage

Zone
A defensive pass coverage where defensive backs and linebackers are assigned areas of the field to defend

"Occasionally I'll deliberately play the role of Joe Namath, football hero, or Joe Namath, TV guy. If people get a kick out of it, if I can help make them happy for some part of time, then I'm happy to do it."

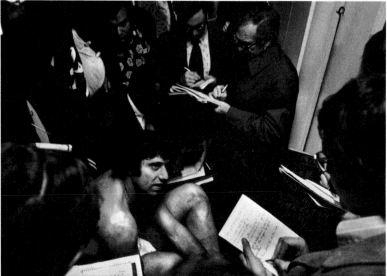

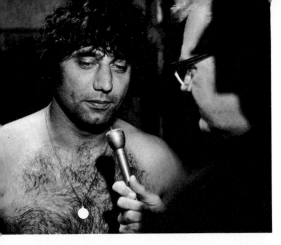